Sales Force Incentives

The Institute of Marketing

Marketing means Business

The Institute of Marketing was founded in 1911. It is now the largest and most successful marketing management organisation in Europe with over 20,000 members and 16,000 students throughout the world. The Institute is a democratic organisation and is run for the members by the members with the assistance of a permanent staff headed by the Director General. The Headquarters of the Institute are at Moor Hall, Cookham, near Maidenhead, in Berkshire.

Objectives: The objectives of the Institute are to develop knowledge about marketing, to provide services for members and registered students and to make the principles and practices of marketing more widely known and used throughout industry and commerce.

Range of activities: The Institute's activities are divided into four main areas:
  Membership and membership activities
  Corporate activities
  Marketing education
  Marketing training

SALES FORCE INCENTIVES

How to use them to increase sales

George Holmes
and
Neville Smith

HEINEMANN : LONDON

William Heinemann Ltd,
10 Upper Grosvenor Street, London W1X 9PA

LONDON   MELBOURNE   JOHANNESBURG   AUCKLAND

First published 1987

British Library Cataloguing in Publication Data
Holmes, George
  Sales force incentives : how to use them
  to increase sales.
  1. Sales personnel – Salaries, commissions, etc.
  2. Incentives in industry
  I. Title   II. Smith, Neville
  658.3'225   HF5439.7

ISBN 0 434 90743 X cased
       0 434 90744 8 paper

Printed in Great Britain by
Redwood Burn Ltd, Trowbridge

Contents

Introduction

Personal selling is a remarkably important component of corporate activity. The point has been made many times, by many people that, in business, nothing happens until a sale is made. It has also been said on countless other occasions, that without a customer, a business cannot exist.

In a small business, it is very difficult to escape this understanding. The scale of events is such that each customer is a known individual and the interface between the supplier and the buyer is very close. Both management and employees are acutely aware of the company's dependence upon its customers and usually take pains to foster good relationships with them.

The importance of the customer is, of course, equally well recognized in larger businesses. But the larger company does have a problem. For as companies have grown larger, it has become possible for many employees to become isolated from the cutting edge of commerce, to the extent that the customer is a distant (and sometimes unwelcome) figure in their corporate lives. It is not that the average employee is hostile towards the needs of the company's customers, rather the problem is one of indifference. Put simply, their tasks are so remote from the customer interface that they have no understanding whatsoever of how the money, that pays their salary, is earned.

At lower levels of organization, misunderstanding of this sort, while not desirable, is usually not damaging. However, if it occurs at higher levels of management, then the potential for corporate self-inflicted injury becomes very real indeed. It is here that the problem lies.

It would appear that many senior staff in large organizations (especially those operating at the strategic level of decision making) have no experience at the customer interface and simply do not understand how personal selling functions. For example, we have noted with interest, how frequently corporate planning is conducted in the absence of any real discussion with the sales force. At the giddy heights of corporate decision making, growth plans are established, human resource estimates developed, forecasts calculated and budgets finalized. The plan is approved, the *i*s are dotted and the *t*s are crossed, yet one simple point is overlooked again and again. A point so basic that one wonders how it can ever be missed. It is this. If the planned objectives are to be achieved, then success will invariably hinge on the extent to which each individual member of the sales force is prepared to work at exceptional levels of performance.

In many companies it is taken for granted that the sales force will do just this. That they will work longer hours, strive harder and creatively develop new and original presentations, simply to fulfil the grand design, so that credit is reflected upon the planners and the lot of every other employee in the firm is enhanced. All this from a humble sense of obligation, without any thought of personal benefit or reward.

The fact that no other member of the company would go to

such lengths, without some incentive being offered, is seldom considered. A human resources blind spot appears to exist when the corporate gaze settles on those responsible for selling effort. Yet, if exceptional levels of performance *are* achieved and the company's objectives *are* accomplished, then it seems fair and reasonable that the salespeople, responsible for that achievement, should be rewarded for their efforts. They, *too*, should share in the company's success.

This book is concerned with the development of such rewards. It aims to explain the logic underlying incentive planning and illustrates how incentives, not only motivate the sales force to greater effort, but result in the objectives of the business being achieved.

George Holmes
Neville Smith

PART 1

The conceptual framework

This book is set out in three parts. Part 1 consists of three chapters which provide background knowledge and outline the general process of designing incentive plans.

Part 2 builds an example of an incentive plan, and makes several detailed observations on incentive plan design. The example will, hopefully, help readers to design a sales incentive plan of their own.

Part 3 contains several worksheets essentially for the reader's own use.

ONE

Introduction to sales incentives

If we consider marketing from an operational viewpoint, then one is obliged to accept that personal selling is one of the four basic elements that go to make the promotional mix. The other three are, of course, advertising, sales promotion and publicity. In turn, the 'promotional' mix is one of the four Ps that constitute the marketing mix; with the 'product' or service mix, the 'pricing' mix and the distribution or 'place' mix making up the other three. Many practitioners insist (with very real justification) that there is a fifth P that has to be considered, the fifth P being 'profit'. Going one step further, the marketing mix in its turn is one of two quite separate but interrelated decisions that along with the choice of target audience (or market) form the constituents of the strategic decision. These various aspects of organizational activity, and the relationship that exists between them, can be illustrated with some elegance by structuring them into a model of the marketing process (Figure 1).

Viewed as part of this model, personal selling appears to be little more than a minor element of total marketing effort, ranking alongside advertising, publicity and sales promotion

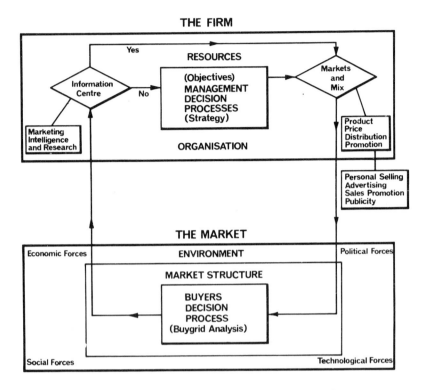

Figure 1

and having about the same degree of importance. The results of research going back a long time, however, suggest otherwise and it is known that personal selling is a key element of organizational success. Even early studies[1] indicated that professional buyers, for example, saw the salesperson as their most important source of information and advice on products and services. Recent updates of these studies suggest not only that the original findings still hold good, but can be generalized over different countries across the world.[2] Of greater interest is the fact that the majority of sales directors in industrial organizations still report directly to top management rather than via the marketing department.[3] Further-more, despite the generalized move towards the marketing concept that has taken place over the last several decades, a surprising number of very successful organizations (such as IBM) still maintain and emphasize a very strong selling orientation.

Curiously, despite its importance, the manner in which personal selling works is still not understood. While innumer-able texts have been written on the 'art of personal selling', most, on inspection, turn out to be essentially inspirational and as such, contain little objective content.

What often seems to be missed is the 'magic' by which one individual is able to create a sale by his or her own creative efforts (which would not otherwise occur), while another person cannot. This lack of understanding of *how* the personal selling process works is one of the last great frontiers facing marketing and nothing like enough research effort has been, or is being, devoted to this tremendously important aspect of business.

The task of selling is to communicate and persuade. In essence, therefore, the salesperson is a 'personal persuasive communicator'. The fact that the individual uses a 'personal' approach is very important, because the greatest single ad-vantage that personal selling has over the other components of the promotional mix is its flexibility. The other elements of the promotional mix (i.e. advertising, sales promotion and publicity) are fixed and rigid. They *can* be changed of course, but to do so takes time and can cost considerable amounts of money. The salesperson, however, by carefully exploring the prospect's needs and wants, and by making use of empathic ability, can creatively alter a presentation to home in and make a sale.

If personal selling is brought right down to basics, then the job of the salesperson is to shift or alter attitudes. Acting almost as a lay psychologist, a good salesperson will work towards changing attitudes from unfavourable towards the company and its products or services, to so favourable that the buyer elects to buy. This is creative selling at its very best, and when carried out by well-trained and highly motivated salespeople, possessing an 'urge to succeed', is very impressive to see. Without the basic 'urge to succeed', stimulated perhaps by well-structured incentives, it is unlikely that many buyers' attitudes will be changed, or that many extra sales will be made.

This book is concerned with assisting managers to develop the 'urge to succeed' within their sales force. It involves motivating salespeople to stretch themselves via the use of incentives, to persuade them to generate additional sales that would not otherwise be made. Sales incentive planning is not a widely understood management technique, yet intelligently used, it can assist sales managers and others to achieve targets and objectives over and above those generally accepted as norms.

Throughout the world of business a great many incentive plans are in daily use. The wide variety reflects the different social situations involved, the different needs of different businesses, and the different philosophical views that prevail regarding the use of rewards. It is not the purpose of this book to suggest a single style of incentive scheme, or even a particular approach. Rather, its purpose is to provide perspective, guidelines and examples that may be of use to designers and users of incentive plans.

It is important to stress at the beginning the importance with which incentive plans should be viewed. Throughout industry and commerce, there is a widespread acceptance that salespeople should be adequately trained and properly compensated. There is also some recognition that offering properly structured rewards can have a positive impact on sales performance. Less well accepted is the view that exceptional selling effort should justifiably result in additional rewards for the salespeople involved. Too many sales managers (it would appear) regard exceptional performance as a 'right', or perhaps even an 'obligation' that salespeople have to the firm. Yet, the payment of additional rewards to the people who were responsible for generating exceptional performance is all too often not even considered.

It is most important that business managers recognize and reward exceptional performance by salespeople. Good managers should be alert to the fact that the provision of a well-structured and effective incentive scheme can result in a stretching effect that generates additional sales of the right products, reinforces marketing strategies, strengthens promotional activity, causes other business objectives to be met, and impacts positively on the growth objectives of the firm. Where successful 'stretching' of this kind occurs, then it should be rewarded by additional payments or rewards to the people who caused it to happen. This is a necessary response, because exceptional performance provides payoffs and advantages, not just for the company, but for every other employee within the firm. For this reason alone, it should be encouraged.

The example set out in Part 2 of this book is equally suitable for large or small companies. In many cases, the design of an incentive plan is greatly simplified in smaller firms. Unfortunately, smaller firms often fail to recognize this and tend to settle for simpler and less effective incentive schemes than those that might be used. It is hoped that this book will overcome such problems and assist sales managers to recognize new opportunities for motivating their salespeople to achieve better results.

The material in this text has been put together using a 'how to' format, so that it can be used as a tool for incentive planning. Printed worksheets are referred to at appropriate points and the reader is guided in their use. Working through these sheets from the text will help the planner to design and administer his or her own incentive plans.

References

1   Gordon Brand and Farrokh Suntook, *How British Industry Sells*, IMR, London, 1977, pp. 9–10.
2   P. Banting, D. Ford, A. Gross and G. Holmes, 'Generalisations from a Cross-National Study of the Industrial Buying Process', *International Marketing Review*, Winter 1985, pp. 64–74.
3   P. M. Banting, D. Ford, A. Gross and G. Holmes, 'Comparative Industrial Buying Patterns in High Level Economies', *Industrial Research*, ESOMAR Congress, Barcelona, August, 1983.

TWO

Motivation and incentive plans

Why have an incentive plan anyway?

The answer to this question may seem to be perfectly obvious. When the question is put to practising managers, however, it invariably results in some hesitation, followed by a variety of responses that seldom reflect any kind of logical stance. What seems to emerge is a sense of uncertainty regarding their organization's motives in using an incentive plan in the first place. It seems fairly clear that in many cases an incentive plan exists for no other reason than long-standing tradition, that represents little more than mechanistic thinking within that firm. Sometimes managers answer the question using mechanistic assertions themselves, with statements such as 'Well, we've always had one for the sales force', or 'It's to help us to achieve our budget'.

It is obvious that neither of these statements represent very good reasons for using an incentive plan. The second clearly has more merit than the first and is a great deal nearer to the mark. But, it still displays a major weakness in the sense that it fails to relate the statement to the salespeople involved, even though these are the individuals who will be most affected by the plan. Now, this is a most important point because if managers are able to present their reasons for using an incentive plan, without considering the salespeople who are intended to be influenced by it, then a critical element of management thinking is missing.

A better answer to the question, of course, would be 'To stimulate the individuals in the sales force to do something that they would not normally do without the attraction of the incentive that is being offered'. Notice how this statement involves the salespeople as part of the definition. If one wanted to be even more specific, then the statement might read:

> *To offer representatives or salespeople a reasonable and attractive reward in exchange for achieving or exceeding some desired previously agreed objective.*

Notice how this version of the definition sets out the real reason for incentive planning. And in doing so, it has also presented us with a problem. A problem that can be expressed very succinctly with two very simple questions. What is meant by 'attractive' and what is meant by 'reasonable'? The answer, of course, is that it all depends. It depends, in fact, upon an enormous range of contributory factors, which do *not* simply revolve around the size of the reward that is being offered; but, more importantly, deeply involve the motivational forces inherent in that particular situation. An incentive is a potential reward. Any incentive that is offered therefore, *must* be perceived to be appropriate to the task in hand and sufficiently large to motivate the salespeople to strive for it. The size of the reward is important. It is entirely possible that too big a reward may be perceived as inappropriate, or suspiciously large, even to the lucky person receiving it. If this is so, then it is clear that a smaller reward, or a different kind of reward (which might be non-monetary), might have provided precisely the same level of motivation. In other words, the 'urge to succeed' may be stimulated by a number of things, of which, money may or may not be the most significant.

Salespeople *appear* to be motivated by such things as responsibility, the opportunity to make a contribution to total selling effort, a sense of freedom, challenging situations, or even, perhaps, by the act of achieving the sales target that was set for them. Any, or all of these things, can play a part in generating the 'urge to succeed' and despite the millions of words that have been written on this subect, it is just not possible to simply set down a list of 'motivators' with any degree of certainty.

What is motivation?

Motivation is a very difficult concept to describe. A starting point is to consider it as a driving force within the individual. It can be thought of as having two forms: positive and negative. Things that the individual needs, wants or desires may be regarded as positive forces urging the person towards some goal. Things that the individual fears or has an aversion to are generally perceived as negative forces that repel the individual away from a particular situation, or a certain set of conditions.

Consider a tennis player for example, who has a burning ambition to become a champion. That person will exhibit dedicated behaviour that will take many forms. These might be typified by such things as endlessly practising, making enormous financial sacrifices, entering a seemingly endless series of tournaments and so on, all at great personal cost to self and family. That person is motivated. But, if you were to ask that person about his motivation, he may or may not admit to possessing such an overwhelming ambition.

By comparison, another player may assert that he *wants* to become a champion, even though he does not *act* in a way that suggests that he will ever achieve that goal. His behaviour suggests, in fact, that he is not as strongly motivated as the dedicated player and as such, he is unlikely to succeed.

Behaviour is the best evidence that we have regarding a person's motivation. The first player we mentioned will keep on working and trying until he ultimately becomes the champion, or until a level of attainment is reached that provides him with the degree of self-actualization that he requires. The player is then rewarded (as a result of his achievement) with widespread recognition and also perhaps by the monetary gains that are usually associated with championship status. Only when the reward is manifest and has become apparent can we start to recognize the motive, for at that point it is very clear that a need has been satisfied.

The concept of needs includes safety and comfort and also involves both physiological and psychological drives. To some extent psychological drives can be thought of as things that people learn as part of growing up in a particular culture or society. In the case of our tennis player, that person had to learn that recognition (achieving the championship and/or money), provided an intensely satisfying reward for his drive. If a general recognition of his superior performance failed to provide him with a reward, then that person would never have persisted towards his goal. In other words, he would not have been motivated.

Motivation then has two separate but interrelated parts. Drives (that state of tension that can be satisfied via some object or some activity); and the rewards that satisfy or terminate those drives. Another way of thinking about drives is to consider them as initiating or sustaining forces of behaviour. All individuals (including tennis players and salespeople) are driven by either positive or negative forces as a result of learning which factors satisfy their own particular needs; and which threaten their comfort and security. Drives tend to work hand-in-glove with rewards. If the rewards that are offered do not match up with the drives of an individual, then those particular rewards will fail to produce an 'urge to succeed'. Since the reward is not perceived to be a reward, then it fails to motivate. If drive states exist without opportunities for a person to achieve satisfaction (or reward), then that condition will simply lead to frustration or anger and *not* motivation.

The purpose of an incentive plan is to provide a potential reward to the members of the sales force in return for extra special effort. Unless the incentive that is offered is perceived to be attractive, then it will *not* motivate, nor will it lead to the action that is desired.

Putting these concepts into perspective, it seems fairly clear that the rewards of any incentive scheme must be seen to be 'reasonable' and 'attractive'. In particular, the scheme must be reasonable in terms of the effort that is required otherwise it will fail to motivate. For example, an individual may be persuaded to jump from a fast-moving car in order to save his life, but he is unlikely to do so for $10. Now in much the same way, a scheme must be seen to be attractive when compared to the compensation that is provided for normal effort. If a person is paid $300 for performing what is generally considered to be the usual tasks associated with his or her job, then offering another $10 or $15 a week is unlikely to motivate him or her to double his or her effort. This is a fundamental issue. And what it means is that the concepts of 'reasonableness' and 'attractiveness' should always be kept in mind by managers constructing incentive programs, as well as those who have to assess them.

Job satisfaction

Before proceeding to examine the particular motives that might influence salespeople, or even consider which rewards might be relevant, it is necessary to step aside for the moment and consider the concept of satisfaction. This is a necessary step, as even the most elaborate incentive plan will not work if the sales force is plagued with problems of job dissatisfaction. A prerequisite for an incentive plan to work is that the salespeople are happy in their work, and like their jobs.

Job satisfaction is an important requirement for generating high productivity. Satisfaction and productivity are implicitly related. Greater job satisfaction will invariably lead to better performance. In turn, better performance tends to generate greater job satisfaction. Good managers understand that this is not just a 'chicken and egg' argument, but simply the synergistic outcome of two closely interrelated events. The important consideration to be kept in mind is that if salespeople are dissatisfied, then their performance will be adversely affected.

The essence of job satisfaction can be summarized in a four step model (see Figure 2). This model establishes that the critical step is the *job itself*. It is of little benefit to change the work environment or the compensation elements if it is the job itself that is the cause of dissatisfaction. Since these two are clearly easier to change, many managers fall into the trap of doing so and provide salary rises, or better cars, or even extra assistants. Yet, none of these things can make up for a dreary dissatisfying job. In western countries, the job satisfiers and dissatisfiers shown in Figure 2 have been identified as important modifiers of work behaviour.

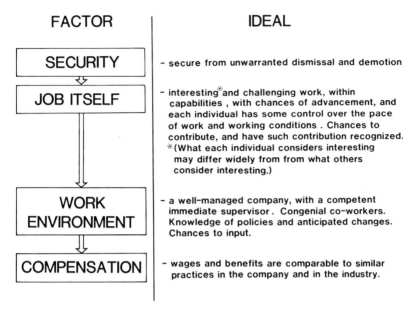

FACTOR	IDEAL

Figure 2

Security

Maslow's theory of sequential development suggests that an individual's wants develop in a sequential fashion, beginning with lower order wants (or needs) and then moving upwards towards higher order wants and aspirations.[1] Maslow's argument (which still holds good) is that early order wants must be satisfied before the next higher level of needs can emerge. Maslow's hierarchy of needs begins with the satisfaction of thirst and hunger, and then moves upward through such need levels as safety/security, belongingness, leadership, self-esteem and self-actualization. The theory suggests very strongly that an individual cannot develop within an organization and achieve higher levels of aspiration until their underlying security needs have been met.

This need is particularly true for lower level and older

employees who find it extremely difficult to develop feelings of loyalty towards the firm and 'get things done', if they lack basic job security and are constantly worried about simply remaining employed. While it is clearly impossible to guarantee permanent employment to every person within the firm, often it requires little more than improved communications to allay employment fears and to provide these people with a greater sense of security.

Opportunity for advancement

While not true of all individuals, a great many people try to better their position in life. Such individuals may attempt to do this by seeking opportunities for advancement through their work. This is frequently the case with intelligent, well-educated people, who feel that they have the ability to make a useful contribution to their organization. Such people will become frustrated and dissatisfied if they are unable to see any opportunities for advancement or progression in their work and this knowledge will serve to act as a demotivator for them. In contrast to this, the mere existence of the opportunity for advancement will often be regarded as a potential reward in itself, and as such, can motivate salespeople to higher levels of achievement.

The company and its management structure

The task of management is concerned with directing the activities of the firm and an important part of this task is to establish effective and efficient channels of communication throughout the organization. If such channels are *not* adequately established, then management will not only have difficulty in achieving its stated objectives, but may well be perceived as being distant and remote by the various members of its own workforce. This can result in employees developing a feeling of 'not belonging', which in turn may cause them to feel alienated and estranged from the people that direct them. It is a basic truism of business that individuals feel little incentive to work hard for any organization if they do not feel part of its structure and communications system. If this is really the case, then management should not be surprised if employees fail to live up to the expectations that have been vested in them.

Communications

The reference to communications within the organization in the previous paragraph needs to be developed further at this point. While 'good internal communication' is seldom, if ever, mentioned when individuals offer reasons for liking or not liking their job, it should still be recognized that 'being heard', receiving 'recognition', and knowing 'why things are done', are all highly important factors for preventing job dissatisfaction. If 'poor communication' is a marked feature of a company's organization and if its workers are uncertain or puzzled about the firm's goals and objectives and their own role in these matters, then this uncertainty will certainly be translated into a reluctance to become involved in activities for which they feel little or no obligation.

Wages and salaries

This particular aspect of employment has considerable potential for creating job dissatisfaction and in turn, for generating the circumstances that could lead to a reduction in motivational drive. Many individuals become dissatisfied if it seems that the salary that they receive is below their level of expectation, is below that of the industry in which they work, or is not consistent with their own perceived level of productivity. If this is a real belief, then the individual involved will become demotivated, will strive less and his or her output will suffer. Even so, it can sometimes be very difficult to strike exactly the right salary balance that will generate both a feeling of satisfaction in the employee, together with an overwhelming 'urge to succeed'. If salespeople *are* paid *above* their salary expectation, this circumstance may well provide satisfaction for them, but there is no guarantee whatsoever that it will result in increased motivational drive. What is needed (it seems) is a salary level that 'satisfies' each person, but still leaves room for additional motivational rewards to develop the 'urge to succeed'.

The job itself

Square pegs in round holes are never satisfied. It is not enough by itself for a person's tasks to be well geared to his or her intellectual capabilities. The job must also fit the individual's own value system (of which self-image and expectations are a part), and fit the individual's interests and/or preferences. The work of Kable and Hicks in the area of 'decision preference analysis' (DPA) has shown the clear relationship of preference to job satisfaction.[2] The DPA provides a measure of an individual's preferences in terms of quantitative (QN) or qualitative (QL), expressed as a percentage split. It also provides a similar measure of jobs against the same criteria. Some examples are:

Consumer salesperson   the job has been measured at 30/70 (QN/QL).

Computer salesperson   the job has been measured at 40/60 (QN/QL).

There is no single *right* QN/QL measure for a salesperson's job; jobs vary from firm to firm. However, the QN/QL measure for a job is easily arrived at, and the DPA profile for an individual can be established in twenty minutes or so. Kable and Hicks's findings suggest that individuals whose QN/QL profile approaches the QN/QL of the job are satisfied, while individuals whose comparative profiles do not, are dissatisfied. In essence, this means that an individual with a 70/30 profile in a 30/70 sales job will be unhappy. The research findings also suggest that there are many such situations.

An incentive scheme cannot correct difficulties brought about by dissatisfaction. It is necessary to correct the job itself before attempting to motivate. The Kable and Hicks research suggests that the QN/QL preference profiles are somewhat permanent in people. But, it is relatively simple to make small changes in the job to improve the fit. It is not possible to take this concept further within this text, and interested readers should pursue the cited reference themselves.

The quality of supervision

The quality of the supervision provided is another important consideration whenever an incentive planner is trying to instil the 'urge to succeed'. The success of an incentive plan may well be a function of the supervisory skill that is available. Good supervisors are able to adapt their own behaviour to take account of the expectations, values and social skills of their subordinates; and to provide supportive supervision as opposed to simply issuing authoritarian commands. Good supervision, intelligently administered, can produce remarkably high levels of motivation and productivity among the members of a sales team. Fortunately, most employees will verbalize their feelings if they feel that their job performance is being adversely affected by poor supervision, so that if the problem does occur, it is relatively easy to spot. It remains, nevertheless, as a potential cause of job dissatisfaction.

The social aspects of the job

Affiliation needs appear to be universal among all people. Individuals do not lead their lives in isolation, but live and work as members of the society in which they dwell. People live in groups, work in groups, relax in groups, are educated in groups and are motivated or otherwise by the other members of the group. Belonging to a reference group and having the social approval of that group is a very basic human need. Group pressures will markedly influence a person's attitude to work. When group attitudes and relationships are strongly associated with good work ethics, then they become very urgent and powerful determinants of personal behaviour. A group accepted goal often becomes a desirable individual goal and can result in friendly, productive and competitive rivalry among the members of the group.

Working conditions

For most employees, the general working environment and the hours of employment involved are not usually causes of job dissatisfaction, especially if the other aspects of their employment conditions are satisfactory. If the terms of employment had not satisfied them, then they would never have accepted the job. Yet, in extreme cases, working conditions can be important. For example, inadequate support (such things as poor sales literature, inadequate samples, or no merchandising) can cause dissatisfaction and result in substandard performance, even when all other aspects of the job are fine. For this reason, working conditions should still be considered as possible causes of demotivation.

Fringe benefits

As a generalization, fringe benefits rate fairly low as a source of dissatisfaction among salespeople. They become important, however, when they are seen to be granted to one group of employees, but not to others, without any apparent reason for the difference in treatment. Good communication of the reason(s) for the difference is usually sufficient to prevent the matter from becoming an issue.

A satisfied salesperson is not necessarily a motivated salesperson. Satisfaction, however, remains a necessary condition if incentive plans are to work. If an individual is free from dissatisfaction in respect of the job itself, then it becomes possible to provide incentives (potential rewards) that can motivate them to achieve exceptional levels of performance.

The visibility of motives

The observed actions of an employee provide a manager with a good indication of that person's motives and the level of his or her motivation. Some of the generally accepted job-significant motives and the factors affecting behaviour, are set out here. These are generally visible phenomena, but readers must undertake the observation and arrive at the proper conclusions themselves.

Achievement and aspiration

The achievement motive is present to some degree in most individuals. Different people have different achievement values, which means that their achievement motives will also differ. The underlying motive for some people may be failure avoidance, while for others the motive might be attainment. The differences that occur may well be a reflection of different achievement values, which may have been learned at an early age in life. 'High-achievers' for example, have considerable confidence in themselves, are happy to accept responsibility and have a preference for clear-cut work situations. They are also willing to take moderate risks in those situations that depend upon their own initiatives and ability.

Closely related to the achievement motive and influential in conditioning behaviour, is the level of aspiration that is present. Aspiration may be regarded as the 'lofty hopes' of an individual, or the extent to which they are ambitious or content. In general, high-achievers need high levels of aspiration for challenging tasks, but not for routine tasks. If people's aspiration levels are unrealistically high and they fail to reach their goals as a result, then there is a strong tendency for them to become easily dissatisfied. The achievement motive can be thought of as the need to see results, to finish, to reach the objective or target. People with a high achievement motive are rewarded by seeing the result.

Affiliation

Virtually every person at some time or other has felt a compulsive need for the company of others. The affiliation motive is responsible for the desire to draw near to other people, and to interact positively with them.

The strength of the affiliation motive differs from person to person. Those with strong affiliation needs tend to be 'people orientated' rather than task orientated, and often respond well to feedback that describes how well the 'group' is doing. In contrast, high-achievers tend to be task-orientated, and respond best to task-feedback that tells them how well the job is going.

Power

Effective leaders are liberally endowed with the need for power. This might be described as the desire to control and dominate others. To compel the actions of other people and to be the arbiter of their fate. Power and prestige are perceived to be synonymous in many societies around the world and can be achieved in a variety of ways.

When an individual possesses a need for power, then there is a tendency for him or her to devote a considerable amount of time and energy, attempting to obtain and exercise that power. The end result may be substantially negative, in the sense that the person may want control in order to dominate others, rather than for the constructive possibilities that go with it. Or it is even possible that the person may have a desire for the symbols of power with no regard for its use. Status seeking is a form of power motivated behaviour.

Power is not of itself a negative phenomena. The motive can be manifested positively, as in the case of behaviour designed to help others and/or to benefit society. Individuals with a high power need seem to enjoy comparative feedback that separates them in a positive direction from others.

Ego

Ego is a factor of personality rather than a motivating influence, but it does bear down upon behaviour. To Asians, 'face' is an important consideration and to 'lose face' is to lose status in society. To western people, 'face' has less significance. But, for many people, 'blows to the ego' can be as painful as physical blows to the body. People often make use of defence mechanisms to protect themselves from loss of ego or esteem and action that avoids threats to another person's ego, can be a means of avoiding potential dissatisfaction.

The visibility of the motives just discussed is complicated by the fact that they exist side-by-side in each person. Each person has a different motive profile made up of a mix of motives of different strengths. It is possible that behaviour that suggests the influence of one motive may, in fact, be a response to a quite different motive. For example, a power motivated individual might seek to affiliate with others in order to have an audience to control; or a social climber might try to mix with, and identify with, those that they perceive to be the socially élite ('status seeking').

The implication for managers of salespeople, is to recognize the range of feedback that is available and required by the different people that they control, and to utilize the type of feedback that best suits each individual.

A special note on morale

The word 'morale' is one that is often used by sales managers to describe the effectiveness of a selling team. High morale is a description used to indicate that a team of salespeople are 'pulling together' and producing good results. It has little to do with the extent to which friendship exists, or that the members of the group exhibit strong affiliation needs. Affiliation and friendship may produce a happy and cheerful group spirit among the salespeople, but it may not lead to group effectiveness.

Morale is associated with the extent to which a group is able to behave in a disciplined and self-confident, positive manner. It is affected by the extent to which an individual within the group is able to accept that the activities and objectives of the group (or work team), are in harmony with those of his or her own. Every individual tends to be influenced by self-interest and will be driven to strive for their own particular goals. However, if that person is also a member of a work group, and given that their joint goals are compatible, it is possible for them to be motivated to participate with that group and work harmoniously towards *its* goals and objectives, in addition to those of their own.

High morale exists, therefore, when an individual perceives him or herself to be a member of a group and also perceives that the group's goals and his or her own goals are totally compatible. This circumstance can occur as a result of the two goals being similar, or possibly because the group's goals assist the individual to reach his or her own. If it is clear that the group's goals and the individual's goals are *not* compatible, then that person's morale may suffer and productivity may fall.

Morale then, is a function of the individual's relationship with the group and is not necessarily related to high productivity. A high-achieving salesperson within a given sales force, may be intensely disliked if the group in general has low-performance goals. Such groups do exist and may be regarded as 'frozen groups', that have as a condition of membership, the maintenance of low levels of performance, together with penalties (social exclusion perhaps) for 'rate-busters'. The authors are familiar with several such groups that have exerted considerable pressure on high-achievers to force them to 'conform'. The same pressure can act equally as effectively to persuade low-achievers to strive to match the performance of a group with high performance goals. The prerequisite, of course, is a cohesive group with strong 'team spirit'. Group cohesiveness can be achieved in many ways. Specially structured meetings and intra-group assistance projects are two common activities aimed at developing a strong team spirit. But well-designed incentive schemes can also assist group morale by providing individuals with an opportunity to achieve their own goals, while at the same time achieving the goals of the group.

Rewards

An individual may come to learn that certain incentives or rewards have the potential to satisfy a number of needs simultaneously, simply because they represent symbols that provide for wider recognition. Money is a common symbolic reward that means many things to different people. For some it represents little more than the things it can buy. For others, it can symbolize power, or represent security, or perhaps provide a comparative basis for them to infer status. For others still, it may represent a proxy that is indicative of a particularly satisfying achievement. Because of the potential breadth of its symbolism, money used as an incentive can be an extremely potent catalyst for influencing performance. It seems clear that human action is aroused by the use of money as an incentive, but the causal relationship between money and any subsequent action is not always clear. Munn makes the point[3] that:

> Money may satisfy the hunger drive by making possible the purchase of food. Its incentive value then rests upon satisfaction of hunger. On the other hand, people who are not hungry, and who do not need additional money in order to satisfy hunger, are still induced by money to put forth much effort in the performance of various tasks. In some instances they are motivated, not by hunger, but by a knowledge of the fact that money will buy clothes which enhance their attraction to the opposite sex. In other instances money has incentive value because it provides a means of gaining prestige, and thus satisfying social motives such as self-assertion and the desire for recognition. This by no means exhausts the motives, physiological, social, or personal, which money may tap.

Money remains, however, the primary reward that an employer is able to offer to an employee. Wallace and Szilagyi[4] reiterate Munn's argument and suggest that money serves at least the following reward functions:

> Money is an *incentive* or *goal* that is highly valued by most employees.

Money is an *instrument* for *gaining valued outcomes* – one can purchase food, shelter, transportation, entertainment, and so forth with money.

Money is a *symbol* that stands for the value of the person to the organization.

Money serves as a *medium of comparison* between employees – my rate of pay relative to yours allows me to compare our relative worth to the employer.

Money is a *generalized reinforcer*. That is, money has been associated through classical conditioning with valued rewards so many times that it takes on reward value in and of itself.

Care is needed when incentive plans are being structured as the power of money to generate greater effort and greater productivity among salespeople differs widely from one person to another. A cash sum that is regarded as being generous to some individuals may well be perceived to be inadequate (i.e. unattractive) to others, with the result that it may fail to produce any significant change in their behaviour. Furthermore, a cash sum that acts as a good motivator for salespeople at one point in time, may lose its ability to motivate them at a later point in time. This is essentially because any monetary incentive that is paid to salespeople on a regular basis, is quickly perceived to be part of their normal remuneration package and ceases to represent a potential reward. In fact, it can be argued that 'partial reinforcement' or, in other words, non-continuous incentives, are more effective in motivating behaviour than those incentives that are regularly applied.

Money is not the sole incentive that may be used of course. A wide variety of other options are available, any of which can represent desirable rewards. Goods and travel may be excellent alternatives to money.

Non-material rewards can be particularly effective, perhaps taking the form of 'overt recognition or praise for work that is well done', or 'the opportunity to achieve a particular target', or 'the chance to out-perform or compete against others', or even the freedom to 'work with a minimum of supervision'. All of these options are valid elements of motivation, *provided* that they are perceived as being reasonable and attractive.

One difficulty associated with using non-material rewards in this way, is that they frequently form an essential part of the behavioural approach used by highly effective managers to stimulate individual or group activity. In other words, non-material rewards are often representative of the long-term behavioural devices used by high-achieving managers to gradually build effective work groups over time. If they *are* being used in this way, then it becomes very difficult (if not impossible) to use them to stimulate extra effort at special points in time. If this is the case, then material rewards may prove to be more appropriate inducements.

Unfortunately, once material rewards are offered regularly on a long-term basis, they soon become regarded as a normal component of basic remuneration. A monthly or quarterly reward paid consistently to every member of the sales force against any continuing criterion, quickly becomes perceived as being an integral part of their normal salary expectation. The inevitable result of this perception is that the reward does little to stimulate greater effort. Of even greater concern however, is the fact that once the reward is established, it becomes very difficult to withdraw even if the performance levels for which it was originally paid are no longer being met. Once the reward has become an expectation, then its suspension will lead to considerable dissatisfaction. The obvious conclusion to draw from this scenario, is that material or other rewards need to be provided on a non-repetitive basis, if they are to realize their maximum motivational impact.

An alternative to this is to offer a more or less consistent reward (which *might* be money) as a sales incentive, but to regularly change the criterion for earning it. If the incentive plan is based upon a changing set of objectives over set periods of time, then every time a change occurs, each salesperson is given the opportunity to assess the 'reasonableness' and 'attractiveness' of the potential reward against the new objective. They are given the chance to re-evaluate the 'value' of the reward, even though the reward remains the same.

The implications for incentive plans

In summary, this chapter has suggested:

- The best place to make any judgements about motivation is on the job. By observing the behaviour (responses) of employees in different situations, one can relate the reward (incentive) to the motives seen.
- Incentives are important as a means of motivating behaviour as they represent socially desirable rewards. While money by itself may not be a strong motivator for all people, it represents a symbolic reward that can be related to a wide range of basic motives.
- Job satisfaction is not necessarily synonymous with high motivation, but it is commonly a prerequisite condition. It is necessary to ensure that employees are happily employed in congenial conditions, before attempting to stimulate them to higher levels of performance.
- Incentive schemes often tend to appeal only to the achievement or power motives of individuals. Some people, however, may be motivated by affiliation, and may require feedback in the form of how well the group is doing.
- Potential rewards offered via incentive schemes must be seen to be 'reasonable' and 'attractive'. The first is related to the effort demanded and the second to the nature of the reward when compared to normal earnings.

If morale is to be used as part of the process of stimulating salespeople to achieve higher productivity, then two further considerations must be discussed.

1 It is necessary to consider the extent to which group objectives (i.e. those that the sales force accepts) are compatible with those of the organization. Both the group and the organization must accept and be committed to the same objectives.
2 In addition, one must consider the extent to which individuals within the group (sales team) have an opportunity to achieve their own goals whatever their basis (status-esteem, ego-gratification, achievement, recognition, or simply earnings), while at the same time, working towards group goals. This means understanding the extent to which individual and group goals are compatible.

From these statements, it can be seen that commitment is an important constituent for ensuring that individual, group and organizational objectives are compatible. One means of gaining this commitment, is to allow individuals to comment on, or to help to establish, the work methods or targets that are intended to be used. This can be done either by working with small groups or by working individually with each of the salespeople. Just which method is used will depend upon the firm. Where such discussions are held, however, it is important not to let too much time pass between listening to suggestions and accepting or rejecting them.

References

1 A. H. Maslow, 'A Theory Of Human Motivation', *Psychological Review*, 1943, no. 50, pp. 370–96.

2 J. C. Kable, R. E. Hicks and N. I. Smith, *DPA, The User's Guide*, NIS Associates, Sydney, 1984.
3 Norman L. Munn, *Psychology: The Fundamentals of Human Adjustment*, Houghton Mifflin Company, Boston, 1961, p. 444.
4 M. J. Wallace and A. D. Szilagyi, *Managing Behaviour in Organisations*, Scott Foresman, Glenview, Ill., 1982.

THREE

Business objectives and sales force targets

The range of objectives that an incentive plan may attempt to achieve will depend entirely upon the needs of the situation at hand. This somewhat imprecise statement seldom presents any problems for planners, as it is possible to structure an incentive scheme to achieve a virtually unlimited range of corporate objectives. Since every company is different and faces different competitive conditions, it is not possible to set down a common set of corporate objectives to suit every situation. So in the course of its daily activities, each company must strive to reach its own particular goals.

Objective setting is a difficult business. Without doubt, some companies select and establish their objectives with consummate skill, basing them upon soundly derived assumptions and a well-researched market position. Other firms establish their objectives with lesser skill, with the result that the precision needed for effective planning tends to be missing. When this occurs, the problem often hinges on too 'loose' a view of what has to be done, so that the objectives that are set down are too broad to be implemented effectively. For example, a loosely stated objective might read:

To achieve the agreed sales target for the whole sales force.

Now, the objective stated here provides us with a useful starting point for this chapter. It is useful, because it illustrates extremely well that the objective stated above, is not an operational objective at all. Rather, it is simply a broad statement of intent. And even a casual examination indicates that far from being a honed and detailed corporate objective, the statement is merely a summary of what it is hoped will happen.

As a summary it is not without value. The broad statement of intent is actually an umbrella that enfolds a number of sub-objectives (or end-purposes), each of which must be spelt out if they are to have any operational value. Notice that it is the successful realization of *each* of these sub-objectives (in a cumulative sense) that results in the company *achieving the agreed sales target for the whole sales force.*

In other words, the broad statement of intent is simply a proxy for the collective achievement of a number of specific corporate objectives. These specific objectives are probably selected because management judges them to be reasonable and worthwhile corporate goals to aim for. Typically, the firm will invest a considerable amount of time and effort before arriving at this position. But what will probably be overlooked in all this planning effort is the *recognition* that the successful achievement of these objectives will probably depend upon the extent to which the sales force is able (or willing) to operate at above-average levels of performance.

In an ideal world, management would no doubt pursue each and every desirable business objective and would hopefully achieve them all with complete success. However, in the real world in which managers are obliged to operate, it is fairly obvious that attempting to achieve too many objectives in any one planning period can dilute *selling effort* to the point where none of them are reached at all.

It is important for readers to note the stress on *selling effort* in the last paragraph because often it is the efforts of the sales force that will determine whether the company's *key* objectives are reached or not. Therefore, good management will carefully select the specific objectives that it can realistically achieve in the planning period under consideration and set the rest aside until a more auspicious time.

If corporate success really is a function of sales force effort, then a prerequisite for good incentive planning is to determine the precise nature of the effort that will be needed to achieve the objectives that have been established. If it is felt that success for some of these objectives will require greater than *normal* selling effort, then the exact nature of the additional effort that will be required should be clearly spelt out in the corporate plan and communicated to those managers who will have to supervise its achievement. It is the recognition that this additional effort is necessary that constitutes the starting point for good incentive planning.

While this may appear to be a somewhat tedious process of thought, the logic of the stages we have just moved through represent a necessary preamble for incentive planning. If it is apparent that exceptional selling effort will be required for the organization to reach all of its objectives, then it seems logical to make it attractive for the salespeople to strive to make these things happen. And this can be done by offering incentives.

From what we have said earlier, if incentives are going to be used to motivate the sales force to strive for exceptional performance, then they must be perceived to be 'reasonable' and 'attractive'. Note that this is not simply a matter of offering cash bonuses. The extent to which a particular incentive is perceived to be reasonable and attractive is affected not only by the nature of the reward itself (e.g. travel, prizes, etc.), but also by the end-purposes that the incentive plan is intended to achieve. Note also that end-purposes constitute those goals deemed to be specific objectives that must be achieved. Some typical end-purposes might be:

To increase sales volume (total)

Incentives aimed at increasing total sales volume seem to ignore at first glance the many differences that exist between the various items in the product mix. Clearly, there will be marked differences in the profitability of the various products, just as there will be differences associated with selling and promoting one product versus another. How then can incentives aimed at improving total sales volume be reconciled with the differences that so clearly exist?

The answer, of course, lies in the recognition that no paradox really exists at all. The fact that a firm uses an overall incentive scheme to increase sales is of little relevance. The additional incentive might be designed to increase the turnover of a major product group, or even to launch a new development. Since action of this sort might be the means by which a firm achieves its key corporate objectives, the use of the additional incentive can be rigorously justified.

Attempting to increase total sales volume is a common marketing objective and tends to be present in many incentive plans. The urge to increase sales is, of course, not unreasonable. It is generally the implementation of the idea that tends to be weak. One finds in practice that certain kinds of incentive appear regularly in incentive plans, often with the same incentive being offered year after year without alteration or critical review. Yet, it is fairly obvious that any monetary incentive that is paid on a regular basis will quickly be perceived to be part of the normal remuneration package. Once this happens, then the incentive promptly ceases to be a potential reward. It is useful, therefore, to occasionally review the components of an incentive scheme against the concept of 'reasonableness', with particular reference to the time period over which the scheme will run.

To increase sales of specific product(s)

Good marketing reasons often exist for wanting to stimulate the sale of particular items in the product mix and several approaches exist for doing this (these will be discussed later). Each different approach, however, has different time-period implications. In essence, the length of time over which the scheme is intended to operate justifies different rewards for different kinds of achievement. This is not an illogical stance as salespeople seem quite happy to accept that smaller rewards for short, concentrated campaigns, are just as reasonable and attractive as larger rewards for longer, more consistent tasks.

To increase sales of a high-profit product

It is a relatively simple matter to tie an incentive payment (or prize) to a special target that has been established for a high-profit product. If this action fits easily into a firm's overall strategy, then the results can be very satisfactory. If it doesn't, then there is always the possibility that it may be counter-productive if the sales of bread-and-butter items are ignored as a result. If the sale of every product in the mix is deemed to be important, but extra effort is needed for certain high-profit products, then this is best achieved by either running a total sales incentive scheme concurrently, or by setting a qualifying minimum sales figure for selected product groups – *before* the extra incentive for high-profit products is paid. In this way, two schemes can be run simultaneously. The first could be a 'balanced performance scheme' aimed at emphasizing particular products in the mix.

Care should be taken to establish just which *products* in the mix really are the high-profit earners. The 'apparent' high earners may not be. So there could well be a payoff from discussing the actual *contribution* that results from each product with the financial controller or company cost accountant prior to developing the plan.

To reduce high inventory

The logistics of stock control sometimes result in situations where inventory holdings are too high and there is a real fiscal need for them to be rapidly reduced. The reasons for such an occurrence are many and varied. The situation can be brought about as a result of forecasting errors, manufacturing over-runs, changes in the market-place, or even the imminent launch of a new, replacement product. It can also result from poor stock rotation, in which case marketing may suddenly be presented with a supply of predated products with a short life that must be distributed rapidly. Specific campaigns based on special incentives can provide a short-term solution to this kind of problem.

To introduce new product(s)

Incentive schemes for this purpose tend to be very similar to those that are intended to increase the sale of high-profit products. We referred to these earlier. However, in the case of a new product introduction there are certain differences that must be noted. In particular, a different range of tasks have to be performed. The high-profit product is almost certainly well-established in the market, trading through effective channels of distribution to a secure customer base. A new product still has to reach this position. If this is to happen, then it will involve a considerable amount of creative selling to the intermediaries in the system before the product can be regarded as being secure. Since new products invariably experience market resistance, additional selling effort will be necessary for the new product to succeed. In turn, this means that additional incentive criteria will be necessary to provide for such factors as gaining initial distribution, acquiring shelf-space, increasing inventory and bringing about increased usage and growth.

To balance seasonal sales variations

Seasonal sales variations are common in many industries, so it is not unusual for firms to experience strong seasonal swings for some of their major products or product lines. Whenever this happens, it invariably results in production cut-backs, increased costs and a certain amount of inventory juggling. In turn, these things lead to inefficient use of plant and equipment and a general run-down in corporate efficiency. If product sales *are* influenced in this way, then special incentives can often help to provide a more even distribution of sales throughout the year. Incentives of this kind can often lead to a significant reduction in production variations and stockholding problems. It is not unusual for schemes of this kind to be divided or split, so that they provide one kind of reward for 'selling-in' and a separate set of incentives for merchandising or 'selling out'.

To gain new accounts

Incentive schemes can also be used to reward salespeople who are able to expand their customer base. New business is essential to the profitable growth of any organization. Missionary calls and pioneering enthusiasm are generally regarded as an essential means of developing new accounts. While there is little argument about the value of this kind of activity, it tends to have a longer, rather than a shorter payoff period – although this will vary somewhat between products and services. This sometimes has the effect of making missionary activity unpopular among salespeople, with the result that they avoid it whenever they can. If this is the case, then it may be necessary to stimulate activity that will lead to an expansion of the customer base.

Schemes of this sort are usually short- rather than long-term and their purpose is to promote extra special effort for a limited period of time. Incentives of this type are usually offered during an otherwise dull selling period. The actual incentives used can be broad or specific to achieve different end purposes. For example, at one extreme it can be based on little more than the number of new accounts that are opened. At the other, the firm may choose to stipulate precisely the size, number and type of new accounts that must be gained in order to earn the reward.

To reactivate 'old' customers

It is fairly obvious that this particular end-purpose is very similar to the previous one. For precisely the same reasons, the incentive is generally offered on a short-term basis only. There are some differences, of course, the major one being that some reason must exist for an 'old' account becoming an 'old account'. It is fairly obvious that if the trading circumstances had been satisfactory, the old account would still be a current account. So unlike a 'new' account, the task of selling to an 'old' account frequently requires additional effort and possibly a plausible reason for the account to be re-opened.

Therefore, it is not unusual for a selling organization to relate this activity to a special product promotion that can act as the trigger for re-activating the account.

To decrease credit exposure

This kind of incentive is often referred to as a 'collection incentive'. Its primary purposes are to:

(a) Reduce the number of 'risk' accounts held by the company.
(b) Lower the amount of accounts receivable from specified customers.
(c) Reduce the overall dating of the accounts receivable, or the number of customers.

Often the purpose behind a 'collection incentive' is to restrain over-enthusiastic salespeople from accepting anything that even 'looks' like an order, especially from companies that have a history of poor payment. Sometimes it simply represents an attempt to reduce a high number of relatively unprofitable small accounts.

Other end-purposes that might be considered could include such things as: improving product knowledge; increasing daily call rates; countering particular competitive action; placing 'point-of-sale' displays; and also, perhaps, for smoothing order rates. Whatever the end-purpose of a business, it is highly probable that an incentive scheme can be designed that will motivate the salespeople to strive for those objectives that they perceive to be reasonable. Listed below is a set of possible end-purposes. Not all of these end-purposes will be relevant for every business and some that are relevant to a particular kind of business may be missing. But the list should be useful for helping sales managers to establish better objectives. This is an important initial first step in designing an incentive plan.

Total sales

Sales of selected products: A . . . . B . . . .
Sales of new products: A . . . . B . . . .
Sales to new accounts
Smoothing sales throughout the year/quarter/month
Revitalizing old accounts
Improving product knowledge
Improved technical/customer service
Better servicing of retailers/distributors etc.
Larger order sizes
Reduced field force turnover
Broader coverage of targeted prospects
More calls per week
Better collections (or reduced accounts receivable)
Better/more timely field reports
Better control of expenses
Better handling of customer complaints
Providing better demonstrations
Making better use of time
Better travel/route planning
Gathering and communicating competitor information
Gathering better territory data
Writing territory surveys
Better vehicle care
Better attendance at trade exhibitions and seminars

It should be relatively simple to rank these end-purposes as objectives that involve and are influenced by the sales force. While all of the end-purposes listed might conceivably represent desirable sales objectives, it is fairly clear that each cannot receive equal emphasis in the same planning period. But whatever priority objectives are selected for the planning period under consideration, it is important to structure the incentive plan to reinforce those particular goals. It is equally important that the same set of goals are established for the salespeople, so that their course of action is established for them. This is a most important point for if the salespeople are to get anywhere, each of them must know where 'anywhere' is. For this reason, each individual needs to be given *specific personal targets that have to be achieved*. Not simply dollar targets, but broad-ranging targets that emphasize particular courses of action and direct the nature of sales.

The progression towards targets

The discussion to this point has concerned itself with a number of important points. First, the nature of business objectives was examined and this was followed by comments concerning the selection of primary objectives in the context of selling effort. The role of the sales force as a tool for achieving corporate objectives was also discussed, as too was the use of incentives as a device for stimulating greater selling effort. The last point of discussion focused on the end-purposes that an incentive plan might be designed to achieve and the fine relationship existing between these end-purposes and the firm's priority business objectives.

It can be seen that a fairly clear-cut logical progression has been developed, starting with a 'loose' statement of intent at the beginning of the chapter and continuing through to the very specific examples of end-purpose that have just been listed. A logical conclusion to draw at this point is that determining priority business goals is not simply a first step towards designing an incentive plan, it is *a necessary step for managing the business and the sales force*.

Furthermore, in determining the specific objectives that it wishes to achieve, a firm is essentially establishing the tasks that the sales force must undertake in the forthcoming planning period. These tasks will then be developed into end-purposes as the incentive plan is developed. The end-purposes that are finally chosen will collectively represent the sales objectives for the entire sales force. Once a clear-cut sales objective has been established, the sales manager now has the task of breaking it down into individual goals for each salesperson on a 'share' or 'target' basis. An individual sales target can be defined as:

A share or proportion that each salesperson contributes to the total sales objective.

The sum total of each salesperson's individual target should add up to the total sales objective or sales target for the overall organization, but should not exceed it. Target setting is often a very controversial aspect of a sales manager's job. It is controversial because each salesperson's wage and standard of living is dependent upon him or her reaching some level of performance that he or she may believe (a) has been assigned in an arbitrary manner, and (b) does not take into account the special considerations that apply to his or her territory. If salespeople believe that their targets have been established in this way, then there will be little incentive for them to achieve them.

In allocating a share or proportion of the total sales objective to each individual in the selling team, it is important that each person is allocated a 'fair share' of the total selling task after taking into account the special considerations and circumstances of each person's competitive situation. Each representative operates in a territory that is unique, with its own problems and its own competitive structure. The special singularities of each area must be taken into consideration whenever individual targets are being struck. The most dangerous error that any sales manager can make is to assume that all territories are equal and that individual targets can be arrived at simply by dividing the overall sales objective by the number of salespeople in the selling team. This action presupposes that a set of *average* conditions exist in each sales territory, a supposition that is not only unrealistic, but one that will be *seen to be* unrealistic by the various members of the selling team.

Selecting targets

The underlying purpose of any target is to improve the overall control of the selling task and to direct selling effort towards end-purposes that are deemed to be important to the organization. Targets are an important part of incentive planning as they provide a focus and a sense of direction for each salesperson in addition to providing a stimulus for his or her motivational drive. If the targets are properly set and represent realistic levels of achievement for each individual, then they not only provide a basis for incentive planning, but also a means of appraising each person's performance over time.

Three principal types of target exist. These are:

1 Volume targets.
2 Profit targets.
3 Task targets.

Volume targets

Sales volume targets are perhaps the most commonly stated targets used in incentive planning. First, because it is an end-purpose in itself, and second, because the principal task of any sales force is to generate revenue. All revenue in the private sector comes from the sale of a product or a service.

There is no other source of money. Therefore, it is logical to measure revenues coming into the firm by the volume of sales that are achieved. Sales volume targets can be specified in a number of ways.

Straight dollar sales seems to be the most frequent measure used, simply because it can easily be compared with the other fiscal measures that form part of each day's business. These other measures might be such things as the salesperson's expenses, or the commission that is due on each sale. Since it ties in so well with other company actions, it is not unusual for sales managers to use dollar volume as a common incentive base. Two advantages are attached to its use: its simplicity; and the fact that it is easily understood by the members of the sales force.

Dollar values, however, change with the passage of time as inflation bites and this means that successive sales years cannot be compared for planning purposes without discounting them back to some prior base year. For this reason, the use of unit measures has replaced dollar figures in a great many industries and this has made it easier to achieve planning continuity. Common measures or unit sizes are now relatively standard and they represent an excellent means of recording on-going sales.

Points targets have always been popular. In many ways, points targets are simply a variation of the unit target system, but they have the advantage of possessing much greater flexibility for controlling the behaviour of salespeople. Their main advantage is that they can be used to direct the particular selling emphasis that a sales manager wishes to achieve for a range of products. Products that sell easily can be allocated a low points value, while those that are clearly difficult to sell can be allocated a high points value. This has the effect of de-emphasizing some of the items in the product range and of emphasizing others. If salespeople have to achieve a specified points target in order to qualify for an incentive payment, then they quickly come to realize that the easiest way to get that incentive is to sell a balanced mix of products.

A further volume target that has gained considerably greater use in recent years is that of the customer target. Merger and consolidation have been a feature of the economic scene in the developed world over the last several decades and the result has been a concentration of buying power into fewer and fewer hands. As an example any seller wishing to contact 80 per cent of the Australian grocery market in the year 1960 had to visit more than 7000 buyers (or decision points). Today, twenty such decision points are responsible for approximately 92 per cent of all retail grocery sales, with further concentration a very real possibility. This is by no means uncommon and similar examples can be drawn right across the world.

In this sort of context, the loss of a single customer can have important ramifications for a selling organization and emphasizes the need for very high levels of sales service. Given this scenario, customer targets represent a useful incentive base for controlling the activities of individual salespeople.

Profit targets

Profit targets serve the purpose of making salespeople conscious of the cost components that are present in all selling activities, together with the need to ensure that sales are profitable. It is not uncommon to find situations where high volume sales make an insignificant contribution to profit, and where the salesperson who is the highest profit earner does not generate the highest level of sales. The fundamental purpose of profit targets, therefore, is to monitor individual sales performance on a basis that has greater relevance to profitability than is provided by simply measuring sales volume. Such targets are designed to produce a sales mix with a better balance, a mix that shifts selling emphasis away from volume sales only, to sales that generate an acceptable return on investment.

Profit targets can be specified in a number of ways. A frequently used method is to establish as a target a minimum dollar profit figure per sale (which is sometimes expressed as a percentage) for which the salesperson is responsible. A variation on this is to set the target on the basis of the expenses incurred in achieving the sale with a maximum spend permitted which is usually expressed as a percentage of the sales dollars achieved. This method is simple and easy to implement, but it has certain disadvantages associated with it. Salespeople with low dollar sales figures (perhaps in a newly created territory) have little to spend in the way of expenses and this can have the effect of making them appear to be less competitive from the customers' point of view. The other extreme can prove to be equally a nuisance. Given a well-developed territory with high sales volume and a correspondingly large expense base, there is a tendency for the representative to spend right up to the maximum that expenses allow, whether the money needs to be spent or not.

A second prime method of establishing a profit target is to base the incentive payment upon the gross margin that is generated by each sale. This is a system that is often used with such products as small goods where the salesperson is selling a wide range of items with widely different gross margins. In cases like this, it is not unusual for the sales manager to average out the gross margin for *all* the products that are handled in the range, and then to set the quota some percentage points higher than the average, as a means of stimulating the sale of the higher gross margin products. The main problem associated with gross margin targets is that the members of the sales force are not always aware of the gross margins earned by each product. This lack of knowledge means that they are unable to work out for themselves the extent to which they are reaching their target. Even if the gross margins *are* known, it involves salespeople in lengthy and time-consuming calculations. For this reason, it is often easier to make use of a points system, for no other reason than it is easier to understand and implement.

A third approach to the problem of establishing profit targets is to make use of net profit figures. These are certainly being used by some companies, but tend to be unpopular with salespeople for precisely the reason bearing down on gross margin targets (i.e. the salespeople have no way of working out how well they are doing). In addition, it is difficult for them to challenge the profit figures that are produced, again because the basic data necessary to undertake the calculation is not available to them.

On the face of it, of course, the net profit target ought to be the best incentive base of all as it depicts so precisely the ultimate end-purpose of the company's efforts. However, because such measures are unpopular and because they are inclined to be administratively cumbersome, there is a distinct tendency for them not to be used.

Task targets

While volume and financial targets have distinct advantages for encouraging the sales force to chase volume sales or profitable sales, circumstances can arise where the drive to achieve these goals can clash with the performance of other activities that are important to company success. A wide-range of activities may have a very real impact on future sales and profits and if neglected at one point in time can act to limit growth in the future. These other activities may represent an essential part of the selling task, but because they appear to provide no immediate payoff, may be brushed aside in the bustle to achieve more immediate aims.

Task targets act to overcome this problem and have the redeeming value of directing the efforts of the sales force towards those activities that are necessary for future corporate growth. These activities include such things as developing new accounts, attending exhibitions, building displays, attending trade meetings or revitalizing dormant accounts. These activities are an essential part of the selling job and have a lot to do with future success.

Such tasks can represent a problem for the unwary, however, as it is difficult to measure the quality of the effort that is put into task-related activity in the short-term. The quantity of effort that appears to have been expended is easily noted, but the value of the effort will only emerge with the passage of time. Where specific activities are regarded as being important to the future well-being of the organization, then task targets represent a useful way of getting these activities done.

The implications for business objective setting

In summary this chapter has suggested:

- Objectives and sub-objectives must be clearly spelt out if they are to have any operational value.
- Determining which of these objectives are to be regarded as priority tasks is a necessary first step for managing the business and the sales force.
- When a firm arrives at the specific objectives that it wishes to achieve, it has essentially established the tasks that the sales force must undertake in the next planning period.
- The extent to which corporate objectives will be achieved, will probably depend upon the extent to which the sales force operates at above average levels of performance.

- If success *is* a function of sales force effort, then the exact nature of the extra effort that will be required should be set out in the corporate plan.
- If it is apparent that corporate objectives can only be reached by exceptional selling effort, then it is logical to make it attractive for the sales force to invest the extra effort that is needed. This can be done by offering incentives.

An example of an unusual incentive scheme meeting a range of objectives

A company in the hardware industry sells a broad range of speciality and conventional products to a diverse group of accounts. Each salesperson is expected to sell the total product range in a vigorous and aggressive manner. To maintain a high level of motivation and to emphasize the sale of particular products, a points target system is used and points are awarded for merchandise sold. The incentive scheme is based upon a sixteen cell matrix (4 × 4) with either single products or groups of products being located in each cell. For every cell, there is a pre-established target made up of 'N' units that must be sold at predetermined prices. The real incentive reward comes from the salesperson selling the *total* range of products. To make this happen, each cell is given a points value that accrues immediately the target volume in that cell is reached. Key products are placed in corner boxes.

If the salesperson can sell a line of products across the matrix (across, down or diagonally), then the number of incentive points awarded is doubled. If the salesperson can sell two lines of products then they get double points for each line. If they are able to reach their target in every cell, then the total points earned is doubled again. The points earned are translated into cash values for each salesperson and the cash amounts are then paid into a department store credit account of their own choice. The salesperson holds the card against which the money is credited and can draw upon it to buy goods or services as and when they choose. It can either be saved to pay for a major purchase, or spent as it is credited.

The company also has an overriding scheme that draws in marketing personnel as well. It is understood within the company that the location of the annual sales/marketing conference is a function of the firm's profitability over the year. If the firm achieves 105 per cent of budget, then the conference is held at an attractive location. The degree of attraction is dependent upon the extent to which the budget is surpassed. People attending the conference are allowed to take their spouse with them, with the firm meeting all expenses. This last initiative is actually self-funding, as achievement in excess of 105 per cent more than covers the cost of the conference.

PART 2

Practical application

Reading a 'how to' document can be frustrating if only a theoretical approach is used. The remainder of this book is designed to overcome this problem. In the chapters that follow, an example of the design of an incentive plan is developed step-by-ste. This will help the reader to follow the design process more easily. To assist further, worksheets are referred to at appropriate times. It is suggested that the worksheets are completed as the reader progresses through Part 2.

The model that is used is derived from the TOPS* Sales Development System developed by NIS Associates.†

* Registered trade name.
† NIS Associates, Sydney.

FOUR

The process of incentive plan design

It is now appropriate to consider the ground rules that underlie the design of incentive plans. In doing so, two key concepts must be kept in mind. These are:

1 The rewards that are offered for achieving specific targets, must be *attractive* and *reasonable*. To ensure that this is so, the principles of motivation set out in Chapter 2 *must* be kept in mind.
2 Incentive plans must be based upon clearly defined *business objectives*, out of which specific *targets* must be established.

The design of a successful incentive plan follows a series of well-established steps or phases. These are set out in Figure 3, and are described in the remainder of this chapter.

Step 1

This phase of the plan is concerned with the selection of a *limited number of priority objectives* that will depend upon the effectiveness of the sales force for their success.

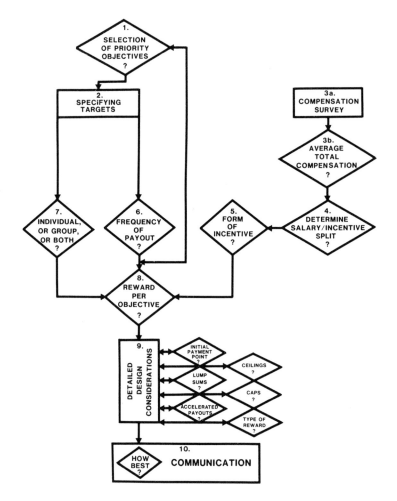

Figure 3   *The process of planning for incentive*

It is important in the planning period under consideration to concentrate *only* on those objectives that are deemed to be vital to corporate success. To attempt to do otherwise will simply dilute the efforts of the sales force, which in turn will reduce the probability that the priority objectives will be achieved.

Those corporate goals that have a lower priority can safely be left until the next planning period, when in turn they may become the vital issues that have to be tackled. The firm's priorities are likely to alter over the period of a year and higher priorities may have emerged by the time that the new action plan is being written. This is always likely to occur in any dynamic situation and will be especially true if a well-written incentive plan has meant that the current priority objectives have been achieved.

Step 2

This phase is concerned with specifying each of the priority objectives that have been selected as *clear-cut targets* to be achieved.

As much as is possible, the targets that are established should be specified for individuals within the sales force and *not* left as overall targets, or as broad statements of intent. There is a clear-cut payoff from converting broadly based sales objectives, to specific targets, which should then be allocated down to each individual salesperson. This ensures that each of them has a personal target to aim for.

If individual targets prove difficult to write because of the nature of the selling task, then small-group targets *may* be a solution. However, managers should be very careful, not to use the small-group target as an automatic fall-back response whenever it appears to be awkward to establish an individual target. If individual targets *are* difficult to write, then one should begin to question the management information system that is being used.

Step 3

In the third phase of the plan, it is necessary to determine the average total remuneration that is paid to salespeople in similar (competitive) firms. Once this figure is known, then it becomes possible to calculate the total compensation package that will be offered to your own salespeople.

An example of the method by which the calculation is carried out is set out in Chapter 5. The important considerations to be kept in mind when undertaking this exercise are those relating to the rules of 'attractiveness' and 'reasonableness'. A compensation plan must be totally realistic. Good managers do not indulge in 'pipe-dreams', nor do they overstate the firm's position. Promising each salesperson potential millions is highly unlikely to be perceived as reasonable by any intelligent person.

Step 4

At the fourth phase of the plan, the decision-maker must determine the manner in which the total remuneration will be split between base salary and incentives. This, of course, must be related to performance at budget or target level.

Remuneration is paid in many ways. Some firms offer a straight salary only, others (as is being suggested here), offer a salary plus incentives. Still others, pay their sales force on the basis of incentives only, using a commission-based remuneration system. This last point, of course, has nothing to do with the subject of this book. Commission only systems can and do work, even if sometimes they only advantage the employer. If the firm intends to use a salary and incentive system of payment, however, then to be effective it should follow the rules of 'attractiveness' and 'reasonableness' that have been the constant theme of this book. Frequently, commission only schemes concentrate on the former and ignore the latter.

Step 5

At Step 5, it is necessary to select the *form* or *type* of incentive that will be used for each component of the plan.

This is really an elaboration of Step 4 and is essentially an accounting issue. This, too, is taken up later in the text (Chapter 7).

Step 6

Determining the frequency of incentive payments.

A whole range of options are clearly available here. Incentives can be paid weekly, monthly, quarterly, or even annually. It is not even necessary for the payments to be the same for each component in the incentive plan. The greatest 'urge to succeed' might be achieved by paying some of the elements in the scheme on a very short-term basis (perhaps monthly), while excellent reasons might exist for withholding the payment of other rewards for a whole year.

Step 7

At this point, the planner must specify precisely the basis upon which incentives will be paid.

The ground rules *must* be set out in advance and the sales force must be told whether the rewards for high achievement will be paid to an individual, or a small group, or a team. This matter was mentioned as an issue earlier in the text when targets were being discussed. The decision that has to be made at this step is clearly related to the statements made earlier. Putting the matter into a nutshell, what can be measured can be rewarded.

Step 8

Step 8 is concerned with allocating a proportion of the incentive money that is available to each specific priority objective.

Sensible managers will allocate most of the incentive money that is available to the more important objectives that have to be achieved. The more a specific objective is vital to corporate success, then the more an individual should be rewarded for successfully achieving those objectives.

Allocating rewards in this way is simply a form of 'weighting', but it does have important implications for directing selling effort towards those targets that are considered to be in the best interests of the organization.

Step 9

Deciding *how* the potential reward will be offered; designing the detail of the plan.

This step requires a number of critical decisions to be made that have a direct bearing upon the likely success of the scheme. The same decisions will also determine the extent to which the various members of the sales force will regard the scheme as being reasonable and attractive. In turn, this perception will also influence how well the scheme stimulates the 'urge to succeed' in each of them.

The critical decisions that have to be made, are actually composed of a range of sub-decisions. These sub-decisions can be illustrated as a series of questions that need to be asked. For example, when should the incentive payments commence? Should there be some achievement level where incremental payments may begin to be earned, *prior* to the target figure, or is it essential for each salesperson to reach the targets that have been established before any payment is made at all. Should ceilings on earnings apply and if so, at what level? If some of the salespeople exceed their targets as opposed to simply reaching them, should they receive an additional lump-sum payment in return for their exceptional effort? What form should the incentives take? Should there be a 'cap' on eligible over-budget sales? Which particular rewards are best – cash, household goods, travel, a better or bigger car?

Clearly, the particular structure of a firm, or the environment in which it operates, will condition the decisions that it has to make. But, the questions listed here illustrate the range of movement that has to be considered when incentive planning is under way.

Step 10

Determining *how* to communicate the plan.

A manager can write the best incentive plan that has ever been written, but the effort will be totally wasted unless the contents of that plan are properly communicated to the sales force. If the sales force are unaware of the contents of the plan, or if they have not been told which of the priority objectives *must* be achieved, then they are unlikely to commit themselves to extraordinary effort. It has to be kept in mind that a crucial part of writing the plan is deciding, as it develops, precisely *how* it will be communicated and presented to the sales force. This particularly crucial 'how-to' is covered in Chapter 7.

The implications for incentive plan design

In summary this chapter has suggested:

- That the rewards that are offered to salespeople for achieving specific targets must be *attractive* and *reasonable*.
- That incentive plans must be based upon clearly defined *business objectives* out of which specific *targets* must be established.
- The total remuneration for achieving priority objectives must be established together with the *form* or *type* of incentives that will be used and the *basis* upon which they will be paid.

- The amount of incentive money available for each priority objective must be determined as must the *manner* in which the incentives will be offered. The overall plan must then be communicated to the sales force.

A reminder

The ideas that have been presented to this point in the book have been developed for the express purpose of establishing a set of principles that are necessary for understanding the behavioural and managerial concepts that underlie the development of incentive plans. The reason for reviewing the material at this point is simply to prepare the reader for the examples that are to follow in Chapter 5. For many readers, the ideas that have been presented so far will be new. For others, they will represent little more than convenient revision.

Whichever is the case, it is now possible to begin developing an example that will illustrate the design of a typical incentive plan. The example will be based upon a set of worksheets, that can then be used by readers to develop their own incentive plans. It is necessary to make the point, however, that the example being developed here is just that and nothing more. As such it forms a convenient guide to incentive planning, but it is *not* intended to represent a model plan for the reader's firm.

An example of a mix of cash and travel as an incentive

A company in the packaged food industry uses an interesting mix of travel and cash equivalent as the basis of its sales force incentive scheme. The company sells a wide range of products both direct to large scale retailers and also to major wholesalers. The company introduces new products each year and a proportion of its other products have a fairly high seasonal factor associated with them. The purpose of the incentive scheme is not simply to motivate the sales force to extra effort, but also to provide the correct emphasis to the new products that are being introduced and to reduce the variations in demand for those products that have a seasonal component. The company employs approximately twenty representatives. Each of them has an exclusive territory that contains a reasonable balance of both large scale retailers and wholesalers. The trading year is divided into four quarters and a points target is established for each individual for each quarter. Points are allocated to each product in the mix. The points value of each product is varied each quarter and in this way, the firm emphasizes the objectives it is trying to achieve. To earn incentives, each representative must achieve the points target allocated to them each quarter.

Incentives actually become payable at 95 per cent of target, but represent little more than token payments at this level. At 100 per cent of target, however, the quarterly payment is $500. This increases to $1,000 at 105 per cent of target and notionally at least, there is no upper limit. The incentive is paid at the end of each quarter in the form of 'Incentive Bonds' – which are essentially cash vouchers that can be exchanged for goods and services in a wide variety of stores.

In addition to the incentive payment, for each 100 per cent of target that is achieved by a representative, the company pays $250 into a travel fund. If a representative hits target each quarter, then $1,000 goes into the fund. The fund pays for ten trips of varying value, ranging from a round the world trip for two, down to a long weekend at a popular holiday resort. To be eligible for a trip, a salesperson must have hit target each quarter. The most attractive trip is awarded to the salesperson with the highest points score that year, the next most attractive to the next highest and so on down. The company asserts that the scheme is very successful and results in over-performance each year with corporate objectives achieved.

FIVE

Specific objectives

In this chapter, the steps set out in Chapter 4 will now be used to take the reader through the design of a typical incentive plan. The plan will be developed on a step-by-step basis as this will help the reader to follow the design process more easily. The reader's attention will be drawn to the worksheets at appropriate points in the development of the design.

It makes it easier to understand the design process if the ten planning steps that are used in the example are kept firmly in mind. At risk of boring the reader, these steps are summarized again as a reminder prior to beginning the example.

The process of planning for incentives

1   Selecting priority objectives.
2   Specifying targets.
3   Determining aggregate compensation.
4   Determining the salary incentive split.
5   Determining the form of the incentive.
6   Determining the frequency of payments.

7   Determining how the incentives will be paid.
8   Determining the reward for each objective.
9   Determining the detail of the plan.
10 Determining how to communicate the plan.

Steps 1 and 2   Selecting priority objectives and specifying targets

The importance of setting sound objectives and targets was discussed in Chapter 3. In this and the following chapter, it is intended to develop an example of an incentive plan using the steps set out in Chapter 4. For the purpose of this example, five operational 'priority business objectives' have been chosen. They have been selected because:

1   They are fairly typical of the kind of priority objectives established by many organizations.
2   They are each dependent upon the salespeople committing themselves to a considerable amount of extra effort *if* the firm's overall targets are to be achieved in a satisfactory manner.

The five priority objectives are:

1   To maximize total sales.
2   To maximize sales of product X.
3   To maximize sales of product Y.
4   To improve collections from 'poor accounts'.
5   To reduce sales personnel turnover.

It will be clear to the reader that in actualizing these five priority objectives, the profit goals of the organization will be achieved.

It has already been stated that it is possible to design an

incentive plan that will act to achieve a comprehensive mix of corporate objective. With this in mind, the example that is being developed here will illustrate how the right mix of components can successfully realize each of the five priority objectives that have been selected. And since it is essential that the plan that finally emerges is perceived to be 'attractive' and 'reasonable' to the people that have to achieve it, this too will be taken into account. The targets for each of the objectives will be expressed in both 'volume' and 'activity' terms and will make up part of the total budget. Alert readers will also notice that a short cut has been introduced. In the example being developed, an assumption has been made that all territories are of equal size. This is simply to reduce any further divisions (which might prove confusing). It does not diminish the value of the example in any way.

Worksheets 1 and 2 should help you to spell out your objectives and targets.

Worksheet 1

Refer back to Chapter 3. Rank your objectives as they involve and are influenced by your salespeople. List below the five or six *most important* business goals for the year ahead *which can be significantly influenced by the representatives*:

1 _____

_____

2 _____

_____

3 _____

_____

4 _____

_____

5 _____

_____

6 _____

_____

It is possible to structure an incentive plan to provide material rewards for achievement of any of the objectives listed above – and, of course, for many others. But an incentive plan which tries to do too much may be confusing. Review the above, and try to restrict the list to three or four.

Worksheet 2

1   Review Worksheet 1. Can all these be stated as targets for individuals (or small teams)?

Priority objectives	Typical target	Available data for assessment of attainment

2   Review your field force/selling force. Which objectives need breaking down as *different* targets for individuals, and which can be similarly (generically) stated? How will you complete this?

_____

_____

_____

_____

Step 3   Determining total compensation

Once the priority objectives have been established, the next step in the design of the incentive plan is to determine the *average* total annual compensation (or remuneration) that it is intended will be paid to the salespeople. This is usually stated as the total remuneration that they will receive for satisfactory levels of performance. Note the inclusion of the word 'satisfactory'. In the context of incentive plans, it means performance at budgeted or anticipated levels.

To determine the appropriate average total compensation for the sales force, a salary survey is necessary. This is really a task for the personnel department and a good human resources manager is likely to be very much in touch with the realities of sales force remuneration. Irrespective of who does the survey, however, it is important to recognize that *all* the elements that go to make up sales force compensation have to be included and clearly established as distinct and separate items. Table 1 provides an example of this.

Using the survey figures in Table 1 as an information base, the planner may decide to use the sum of $21,150 as the yardstick for establishing the average total compensation figure for each salesperson. This figure is actually higher than the true average of $20,985, but an analysis of Table 1 indicates that the true average was influenced somewhat by one low-paying company. The manager developing the plan may wish to be among the better paying companies in the industry in which they operate, although perhaps, not necessarily at the top. (Per diem allowance was not included in Table 1, but in some cases might be an important 'compensation' element to include.)

Worksheet 3 can now be used to complete a compensation analysis of this type.

Worksheet 3

Company	Average base salary	Range of base salary	Average commission	Average quota (incentive)	(Value of) non-cash incentives (trips, prizes)	Total compensation	Extras

Table 1

Company	Average base salary	Range of base salary	Average commission	Average quota (incentive)	(Value of) non-cash incentives (trips, prizes)	Total compensation	Extras
A	17,000	16,000–22,000	—	4000	250	21,250	Car in rural area
B	16,000	15,000–17,000	2000	2500	650	21,150	Car allowance
C	16,500	15,500–18,500	—	2000	350	18,850	Car provided
D	19,000	16,000–23,000	—	1500	—	20,500	Car provided
E	17,500	16,000–19,000	—	2500	1000	21,000	Car allowance/ expense allowance
F	15,000	14.000–16,000	4000	4000	—	23,000	Car allowance
G	16,000	15,000–17,500	3000	1800	350	21,250	Car allowance in some terri- tories

Step 4   Base salary versus incentive pay

The split of total compensation into base salary, incentives and other components depends upon a number of factors. To managers with no field selling experience, base salary always seems to be an equitable means of remunerating the members of a sales force. It seems fair (it would appear) for the salespeople to be reasonably compensated at a fixed level in return for a fair day's work. However, this is an analysis of the situation from a non-selling point of view and while it may well be satisfactory for some salespeople in some selling situations, it is certainly not a universal solution. Highly creative salespeople may well regard a *base salary only* compensation plan as restrictive and tight, offering no opportunity for additional reward for extra effort. As opposed to this, too *high* a proportion of total compensation in the form of incentives or commission may make it difficult to attract sales staff, as in the event of adverse business conditions outside their control (a recession perhaps) the total payments that they receive may seem to be unreasonably low for the amount of effort involved. This might make it difficult to retain staff in difficult times. While examining the factors that bear down upon the compensation split, it is useful to keep the information set out in Figure 4 in mind. The factors that have to be considered are:

- Whenever the competitive situation in which the firm operates in imposes a clearly recognizable requirement for creative personal selling and highly developed persuasive skills, then the incentive component is important and should be high relative to base salary.
- In team selling situations, both group incentives and high salary are equally common.

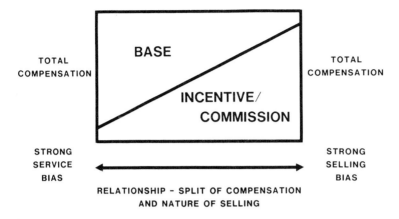

Figure 4

- If customer service and other associated activities are primary tasks of the sales force and demand that the salespeople spend a considerable proportion of their selling day on non-selling activities, then base salary is important and the incentive component should be low.
- If the operational context that the sales force work in is at the high-end of the technology scale and involves them in persuasive communications with highly trained buyers or engineers, then it is important that they possess the technological ability to talk with these people on equal terms. This suggests that salespeople operating under such conditions have to be better trained in the technology than their prospective clients if they are to operate effectively. Given this scenario, then salary will be high relative to total compensation and incentives will be low, but should exist.

In practice, most company compensation schemes are scattered across a range of possible options. The incentive proportion may be as low as 10 per cent, or as high as 35 per cent of total remuneration. The base component usually has to meet some agreed minimums or award conditions in most employment situations.

It is fairly obvious that there is no single right answer to the exact split between salary and incentives. Every organization faces different competitive circumstances and will be trying to achieve different objectives. Yet, it is difficult to imagine that an incentive of less than 20 per cent of total compensation would be perceived as an attractive reward by salespeople, least of all as one that would motivate them to extraordinary effort.

Continuing the example, let us assume that total compensation is made up of base salary and incentives only and that the incentive payments are 30 per cent of total compensation. This would mean that the average targeted total compensation of $21,150 would be made up as follows:

Base salary	$14,000
Incentive payment	$6,350
Total compensation	$21,150

Notice that the sum of $21,150 is the total anticipated compensation to be paid to a salesperson who achieves budgeted or target sales. This, of course, is the figure that *should* be budgeted for a salesperson's compensation. Any incentives that are to be paid for achievement *above* target performance have *not* been included to this point. Sales that occur over and above targeted performance are actually incremental sales. Common sense suggests that any additional incentive should be paid for out of the incremental gain. This is a very sensible approach, because there will always be much greater flexibility available for incentives that are provided for achievement over and above the target.

Worksheet 4 should now be completed. In doing so, be careful to fully consider the service/sales split for the representatives.

Worksheet 4

	Total compensation (from Worksheet 2)	Incentive payment	% split	Base salary
Note: Consider fully the service/sales split of your field force. Use these columns to build up some alternatives.				

Step 5   Selecting the form of incentive – incentive plan alternatives

How should the sum of $6,350 be used to achieve the business objectives of the firm in the best possible manner? At least two options exist.

1   Base salary plus straight commissions, or
2   Base salary plus a quota-based incentive plan.

Straight commissions are unpopular in many organizations, so that quota incentives (perhaps with other associated special awards) are more commonly used. Sound reasons exist for this, as a number of problems are associated with straight commissions. For example:

(a)   Commission only schemes limit territory flexibility. In those situations where salespeople are paid on the basis of the sales volume that they generate, there will be a reluctance to move to smaller or more difficult territories if it appears that their remuneration might suffer.

(b)   Straight commissions provide nothing in the way of a psychological target for salespeople to strive for. Straight commissions reward every sale, but it should be recognized that the act of achieving an agreed target is in itself a motivator. A basic premise of management by objectives is the achievement of targets that have been mutually agreed between the individual and the manager. This approach has been known to produce high levels of performance.

(c)   Straight commissions reward all sales equally. The 'urge to succeed' appears to be generated to a much greater extent by variable commission schemes that have the flexibility to provide better rewards for higher levels of budget attainment.

(d)   Straight commission schemes result in higher 'break-even' points in terms of sales generated than normally occurs with a quota-based system. This fact is illustrated in Figures 5 and 6. Readers might find it useful to discuss the logic of this topic area with an accountant if they are uncertain about the point being made.

In contrast to straight commissions, quota-based systems:

(a)   Provide each salesperson with an agreed target to aim for (i.e. a motivator). The existence of a target above which additional incentives can be earned makes it possible for the salesperson to judge the 'attractiveness' and 'reasonableness' of the rewards that are being offered. An attractive and reasonable scheme will invariably lead to higher levels of performance.

(b)   Quota-based systems provide considerably more flexibility for structuring a range of (perhaps different) incentives, that have the ability to accelerate rewards for performances that exceed budget targets.

(c)   Quota-based systems provide a lower 'break-even' point.

(d)   Quota systems do not reward slow sales, in contrast to commission-based schemes that do. Firms using a straight commission system are obliged to pay the compensation that is due whenever a sale is made, regardless of whether the rate at which sales are being made matches the companies' expectations or not. If only low levels of sales are being made, it is quite possible that the same rate of sales could be achieved without employing a salesperson at all.

Figures 5 and 6 need to be compared graphically as a number of points arise from the comparison between them.

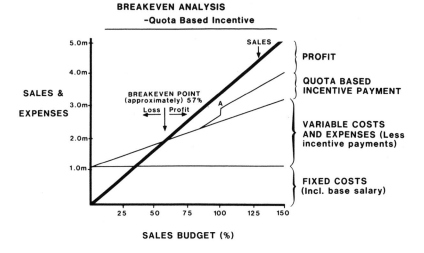

Figure 5

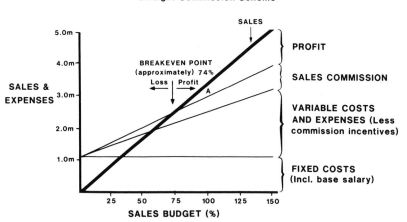

Figure 6

(a)   In each case, salespeople receive equal incentive payments for sales at 100 per cent of budget. Below budget,
the quota scheme pays out less than the straight commission plan, but it rewards 'above budget' performance at a
higher level. Note that variable commission schemes can
be designed to provide payouts very similar to quota
schemes and are a viable alternative to quota incentives.
In fact, the two are conceptually very close.

(b)   At 100 per cent of budgeted sales (point A on the
graphs), profits are the same with either system. At less
than budget sales, however, profits are higher with the
quota scheme. At levels above budget, the graph indicates that the quota system provides slightly lower
profits. This is a function of the increased level of benefits paid to the salespeople. The 'above budget' profit
is slightly misrepresented in both examples, as the
variable costs shown would not continue to rise in fixed
manner that the graphs indicate. The reasons for this
are many and varied. Distribution costs, for example,
do not necessarily, increase as sales rise; they may
well increase at a decreasing rate. Or it is possible that
no new promotional material may be needed as sales
increase.

Step 6   Team versus individual incentives

The sum of $6,350 was allocated as the amount of total sales
force compensation that will be paid in the form of incentives.
Assuming a sales force of ten people, the next logical step
in the incentive planning process is to decide whether the
money should be used to provide individual or team incentives. Option one is to reward the sales force *as a team* for
attaining the budgeted targets established for them *as a team*.

Option two is to reward the salespeople *individually* for achieving the targets set down for each of them as *individuals*.

Worksheets 5, 6 and 7 are useful when considering quota systems. It will probably be useful to get assistance from finance and/or accounting people at this point, particularly if 'break-even' points need to be calculated. In addition, information regarding the contribution of individual products and/or services will also help here. Some examples are given on pages 98 and 99.

If it is possible to get reasonably accurate data on the performance of each person in the sales force, then it is better to opt for the individual method of reward. The majority of companies can measure the performance of each of their representatives fairly easily, and in fact most firms base their incentive plans on individual achievement. Self-interest is invariably present and acts to motivate each person to strive for targets that are clearly in their own best interest. Well-conceived incentives will certainly act to motivate each individual to achieve or exceed their personal targets.

However, individual targets are not always possible. The structure of a firm's operational context may prevent it from using incentive schemes based upon each salesperson's performance. This can occur in major urban areas, for example, if national distributors cross territory boundaries, or perhaps when a sales force is involved in indirect selling, such as happens in the case of ethical pharmaceuticals.

Most sales managers tend towards the use of incentives directed to individuals rather than awarded to the sales force as a whole. If a manager experiences difficulty in measuring individual performance within sales territories, then it is usually possible to use the next larger organizational unit in the sales force. This could well be a district team made up of just a few people. By using the smallest feasible selling unit, it is possible to retain the feeling of personal involvement, so that each individual believes that his or her contribution is an important element in the group's success. If individual incentives are not possible, then, structuring groups made up of just a few people means that the achievement reward relationship is still a close personal experience, so that the motivational impact of the incentive is retained.

Worksheet 5

The following 'break-even' graph outlines (Worksheets 6 and 7) may be useful here. You could also ask your finance and accounting people to help you use this as a guide to assist you.

Consider the following:

Straight commission ('agents')   Your thoughts?

....

....

....

Base salary, plus straight commission.   Your thoughts?

....

....

....

Base salary, plus quota-based incentive plan.   Your thoughts?

....

....

....

Other alternatives?

....

....

....

Worksheet 6

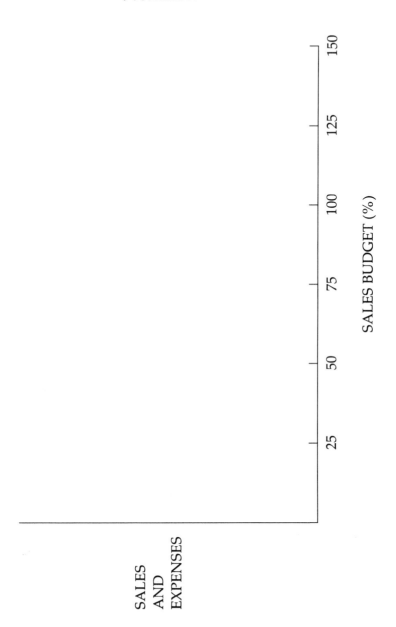

BREAK-EVEN ANALYSIS – STRAIGHT COMMISSION SCHEME

SALES
AND
EXPENSES

25 50 75 100 125 150

SALES BUDGET (%)

Worksheet 7

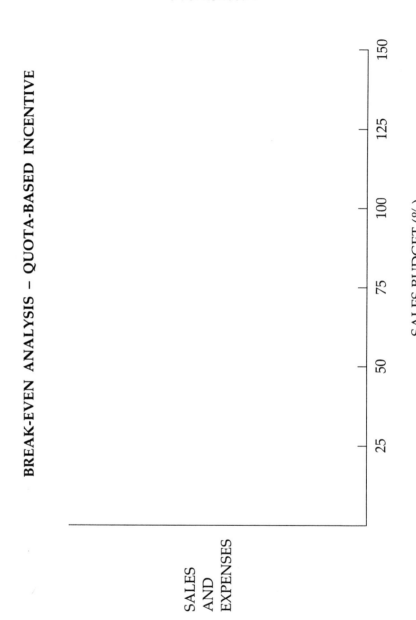

BREAK-EVEN ANALYSIS – QUOTA-BASED INCENTIVE

SALES AND EXPENSES

SALES BUDGET (%)

25   50   75   100   125   150

Step 7 Frequency of incentive payments

Once the team versus individual incentives decision has been made, the next logical step in the incentive planning process is to determine *when* the incentives should be paid. Seen from the firm's point of view, the purpose of the incentive plan is to motivate the sales force to exceptional levels of performance, to ensure that they achieve the year-end total budget. Just *when* incentive payments are made has a distinct impact on the 'urge to succeed' that is generated among the salespeople. The shorter the time interval between reaching a target (even if it is only an intermediate target) and the payment of the reward, the stronger the impact of the incentive on perfor- mance. There is a very real synergy between the thrill of successfully achieving a target and the satisfaction of receiv- ing the reward. The two act together to produce a remarkably strong motivational drive.

Short payout periods often have the advantage of appear- ing 'reasonable' if salespeople experience adverse conditions in any one incentive period. If an individual has not been too successful in a particular incentive-period, then a short payout period allows them to 'start again' without incurring a penalty that makes it almost impossible for them to recover.

If incentive payouts are too frequent, however, then they result in all sorts of administrative difficulties and expense and can prove to be a disincentive rather than a motivational plus. If incentive payouts are *too* frequent (say, monthly), then they may result in payments that are so small that they are not perceived as being sufficiently 'attractive' to merit extra effort.

Long payout periods have problems as well. Even if the payouts are significantly large, if the time period before they are paid is excessive then there will be a tendency for moti- vation to fall off during the long run-up to the payout date.

If the quota period, for example, is twelve months, then the rewards for effort and high performance in the first months of the year will not be seen until the end of the year. The quarterly incentive period overcomes this problem. It is short enough to be seen as 'reasonable', but long enough to produce incentive payments that are large enough to be 'attractive'.

Even so, the quarterly period has its own problems and can provide opportunities for sales to be manipulated to the firm's disadvantage. If a representative is not prepared to sustain selling effort consistently over time, then it is possible for him or her to manipulate the sales figures to produce alternatively good and poor periods unless management can monitor activity and results comprehensively, which, of course, it should be doing. This unruly behaviour can have the effect of producing an incentive payout every second period without the need for extra effort. Uneven sales patterns of this sort are in conflict with virtually every firm's objectives and make little contribution to high performance. Since firms are interested in consistent, predictable performance against set objectives, the possibility of manipulative behaviour from an unruly representative emphasizes the need for carefully balancing the payout periods. One possible solution is to cap quarterly incentive payouts at 110 per cent of quota, with extra earnings carried over on a year-to-date (YTD) basis, or used as credits for future quarters if the 110 per cent cap is not reached. Several advantages accrue from this approach.

(a)   It acts to prevent sales figures being manipulated to gain an incentive without extra effort.
(b)   It minimizes the payout of 'windfall' sales.
(c)   It provides a year-end 'bonus' for very high performers.
(d)   It acts to retain top salespeople throughout the year, as the YTD incentives that have been accumulated are only

payable if the people concerned are still on the payroll at the end of the year.

(e)   It permits the year-end reward to be of a different nature than the quarterly incentives and causes them to be seen as a major carrot.

Properly designed quarterly payouts also provide sales-people with the opportunity to start earning incentives afresh if their early results happen to be poor. If a salesperson's motivation to work towards extraordinary performance is diminished by having to overcome a disastrous start, then the incentive scheme will have significantly less motivational impact.

Worksheet 8 will help you to relate your ideas on 'team vs individual' and 'frequency of payout' to your own situation. Try this before continuing.

Each of the five objectives set out at the beginning of the chapter will now be examined to decide how the incentive components that relate to them should be structured.

Step 8   Allocating incentive money to priority objectives

Objective 1   To maximize total sales

The component intended to maximize total sales will be based on an individual quarterly payout scheme, but with a quarterly incentive carry-over provision that will yield an annual reward on a YTD basis. This will be called Component 1 of the plan.

Objectives 2 and 3   Maximizing sales of products X and Y

Two of the priority objectives that were established are concerned with ensuring that sales of Product X and Y improve

Worksheet 8

Individual vs team

Preference? ....

....

....

What's practical? ....

....

....

Opportunities for both? ....

....

....

Frequency of payout   Simply record your thoughts here before proceeding with any detailed design:

....

....

....

....

....

substantially in the forthcoming planning period. In order to effect these aims in line with the plan, Product X will be the focus of major markcting effort in the firsl and third quarters of the year, while Product Y will be heavily promoted during the second and fourth quarters. To reinforce selling effort during each of these quarters, a 'special product incentive' will be used. This special incentive will be referred to as Component 2 of the plan. Sales of Products X and Y will earn two different kinds of incentives. The first will be a reward based upon the total sales that each individual achieves, which includes X *and* Y. The second will be a special incentive for *each* of these products. The incentives that are available from the sale of these two products will be a significant feature of the overall reward that each salesperson will receive, as both X and Y generate high contribution. The fact that extra incentives are being paid to ensure that the targets for these products are achieved is perfectly reasonable.

Objective 4   Improving collections

A further priority objective is to improve the firm's accounts receivable position. Throughout the year, the ten salespeople will be asked to make a special effort to collect from and/or encourage early payments from selected accounts. This will be referred to as Component 3.

Objective 5   To reduce sales staff turnover

Positive steps will be taken during the year to hold down staff turnover by the use of a YTD incentive. This YTD incentive will only be paid to those individuals who are actually on the payroll at the time that the payout is made. This will be called Component 4 of the plan.

Each of the priority components that have been selected

will be weighted to rank the importance of each to the company. The weightings chosen for the purpose of this example are set out in Table 2. This table also illustrates how the $6,350 (that has been established as the incentive that will be paid to achieving 100 per cent of budgeted sales), will actually be used.

Table 2

Component of plan	Description	Weight	Budget	Per person potential reward at budget level	
1	Total sales	10	32,000	(4 × 640 + 640 annual)	3200
2	Product X/Y	8	21,500	(4 × 537.5)	2150
3	Collections	3	10,000	(4 × 250)	1000
		Total	63,500		6350

Component 1 (total sales)

This component will consist of four quarterly incentive payments of $640 each, with an additional payment of $640 at the end of the year for those salespeople who achieve the total sales target. Disregarding any sales above the set budget for the moment, these potential rewards will provide an end-of-year payout of $1,280 (last quarter plus YTD) to each representative that achieves the targets. This sum should be sufficient to strongly emphasize the plan throughout the year. To protect the last quarter and to retain a sufficient end-of-year emphasis, it might be necessary to consider 'caps' and/or 'carry over' options before the design of the plan is fully completed. Note also that the influence of these initiatives will have a substantial impact on Component 4 of the plan.

Component 2 (special products)

This component will consist of four separate, quarterly campaigns, each of which will offer incentive payments of $537.50

for those salespeople who achieve 100 per cent of target performance. In order to qualify for any of the rewards associated with Component 2, it will be necessary to qualify for Component 1 in the same quarter. This provision is intended to ensure that a balanced sales effort is achieved from each member of the sales force.

Component 3 (collections)

In all four quarters, each of the representatives will be provided with a list of five selected accounts. Since there are ten representatives in the sales force, this means that the firm will be focusing its attention on a total of 200 customer accounts during the course of the year. Each salesperson will be expected to make a 10 per cent gain in accounts receivable by the end of each quarter. This gain will be measured on the basis of the dates on which the accounts are paid. A representative can achieve this target by either reducing one account substantially, or each of the five accounts by some amount. Each individual will receive $25 for every 1 per cent gain. This particular incentive is intended to run for one year only. Whether or not it is permitted to run beyond the current year will be a function of its success during the present planning period. In the normal course of events, this last point would not be communicated to the sales force, otherwise the last quarter of the year could see some very heavy selling to a rash of dubious accounts.

The overall objective of Component 3 is to gain a total reduction in accounts receivable (of 37 per cent in dollar terms), for accounts older than sixty days. Since it will become progressively harder to achieve the target for this objective as the year moves on, the five accounts allocated to each salesperson will be largest in the first quarter (approximately 10 per cent of the original dollar total) and the five in the fourth quarter will be somewhat smaller (approximately 7.6 per cent of the original dollar total). As the salespeople are paid on the basis of the percentage gain that they achieve, the absolute size of the account does not affect their incentive.

Component 4 (staff turnover)

This is relatively simple to structure and will simply consist of the requirement that an individual has to be on the payroll at the time that the YTD payments are being made, *if* they are to receive any of the end-of-year rewards. While it is important to make certain that any payments that are due are paid to the individuals that have earned them, it is quite valid to retain YTD payments if this condition of employment has been carefully communicated in advance. The issue becomes particularly significant at the end of each planning year when substantial cash payments may be due to high performing salespeople. Poor performance merits no reward, so turnover of these individuals can be permitted to continue.

Worksheet 9 is designed to help you to weight each priority objective and to break-out reward levels for different components of your plan. Make sure that you refer back to Worksheets 1 and 2 and keep your objectives firmly in your mind.

Worksheet 9

Component of plan	Description	Weight	Budget	Per person potential reward at budget level

An example of an incentive scheme with spouse involvement

A small division of a multinational transport firm decided to launch a new service. The initial success of this service depended heavily on extra effort from the sales force. In particular, this extra effort required members of the sales team to 'work back' for one or two evenings each week.

To help the new service to become established, a new incentive was conceived and announced at a dinner held for the salespeople and their spouses. After explaining the need for members of the sales force to work back on several evenings each week, in order to successfully launch the new service, the general manager told the salespeople that each individual who achieved the monthly sales target in respect of the new service, could take his or her partner to a restaurant of their choice and enjoy a dinner to the value of $100, which would be paid for by the company.

In addition to this, the best sales performance each quarter (over budget), would be rewarded with an all expenses paid weekend for two at locations similar to Chewton Glen or Gleneagles. The overall winner at the end of the twelve month planning period would receive a prize of a two-week holiday for two at an exotic resort.

Every member of the sales force claimed the dinner for two each month and the new service was launched with over-whelming success.

Establishing the rewards

A considerable amount of progress has now been made. To summarize:

1 The general structure of the incentive plan has been established.
2 The total reward that is available has been assigned to each objective.
3 The various components of the plan have been tied together.

It is now necessary to examine the detailed issues that will impact on how *attractive* the plan will be seen to be. Figure 3 establishes the stages of the planning process for developing incentives. This process is of fundamental importance at this point in the text and for this reason it is illustrated again here. It is suggested that readers familiarize themselves with the process before proceeding further.

Step 9   Detailed design considerations
When should incentive payments begin?

Notionally, incentive payments should begin when salespeople achieve 100 per cent cent of the targets set down for

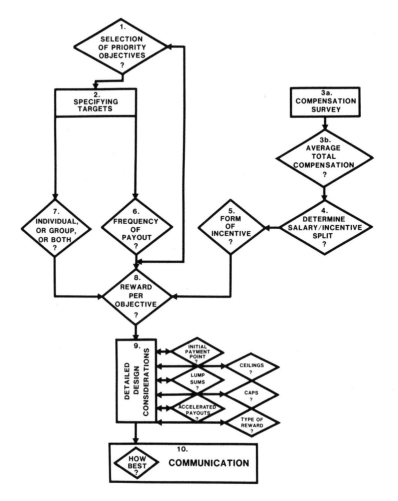

them. However, two good reasons exist for paying incentives prior to this point.

The first relates to the fact that the firm is offering a 'potential' reward that will be paid to each individual when he or she achieves the performance targets that have been set down. Notice that the reward is a 'potential reward', tied completely to target achievement. Good managers will want to make quite certain that the 'potential gain' to each salesperson is fully recognized. And an excellent way of making sure that this happens is to begin the incentive payments at a point below the 100 per cent level, so that, in effect, it whets the appetites of the salespeople concerned.

The second reason for beginning incentive payments early is related to the firm's forecasting ability and the extent to which the quota or target estimates are accurate. Sales objectives are set on the basis of the firm's forecasts of business performance during the forthcoming planning period. With the best will in the world, it has to be recognized that any estimate of the future contains a substantial element of uncertainty. New states of nature will inevitably occur (that can never be predicted in advance), which means that some degree of error has to be accepted.

Given that uncertainty exists, then the question that emerges is whether the salespeople should be expected to bear the adverse affects of this uncertainty. Clearly, it would be irresponsible to expect this, since the targets that have been set down will be inaccurate to the extent of the uncertainty that has been built in. Using Component 1 as an example, given that a 10 per cent error in the quota or target estimates is possible; then incentive payments should begin at the 90 per cent target level, both quarterly and annually.

For precisely the same reason, in Component 2 of the plan, incentives payments should begin to be paid at the 80 per cent level. It is not that the firm is less accurate in its forecasts here, but rather that the salespeople's attention should be focused on products X and Y as early as possible, so that their appetite for achieving the reward is whetted at the earliest possible moment.

The imposition of ceilings or 'caps'

The most important reason for imposing ceilings on incentive payments is to protect the company against the possibility of paying windfall incentives that might be earned without the exertion of any additional effort by the sales force. This could happen in the pharmaceutical industry, for example, if a sudden widespread epidemic occurred and demand became a function of the urgent need for effective medication. Similarly, ceilings can provide a degree of cost protection in those situations where the sales force in general is selling well below target, but one or a few representatives are achieving over-budget results. Since overall sales are below target, costs are not being properly covered, yet the company is obliged to pay incentives to those salespeople who do hit their targets from an eroded profit base.

Note that although ceilings are a useful device for imposing restraints on payments that are not legitimately due, it is possible for them to have a negative affect on sales because of their ability to dampen enthusiasm if they are structured to 'bite' at a point marginally above normal income. If it becomes necessary to establish ceilings in this way (perhaps for a range of fiscal reasons), then it is prudent not to overly stress the fact when the plan is being communicated. If the ceilings that are struck are well above normal income which they *should* be, then the matter is less important and the possibility of dissatisfaction is greatly reduced.

Despite the need to establish caps where organizational requirements dictate their use, one should keep in mind that one of the aims of a good incentive scheme is to stimulate sales *above* the budgeted or target level, simply because of the additional profit that accrues from such sales. From an accounting viewpoint, the contribution that each product generates is partially consumed below the target level in covering fixed costs (including the base salary component of each salesperson's remuneration). Beyond the 100 per cent target level, however, the contribution received from each product is almost entirely converted to profit and as such has a dramatic impact on corporate performance. If ceilings have the effect of restricting sales above the target level, then there is a need for some restructuring to eliminate the factor that is restricting incremental sales.

Over-target performance provides good opportunities for a different set of rewards to be provided, as an additional or overlapping incentive. Much more freedom of movement exists whenever incremental sales are involved and there is a real payoff from relatively generous payments in these circumstances. Examples exist of companies that offer less than 1 per cent of the revenue from over-budget sales in the form of extra incentive payments to the people that generated those sales. By any measure, this would appear to be a remarkably low expense level for such profitable performance. It would be very interesting to consider how such a company's performance might alter if the potential reward was increased to, say, 4 or 5 per cent of incremental sales, and to note how little this increased payout would affect their total profitability.

In the example being developed, it is intended to cap the incentive plan at a point about equal to normal base salary (say, $16,000). This would certainly be perceived as being attractive to a person with a base salary of $14,800. Notice, too, that incentive payments at this cap level will only be received by the *top* level performers within the sales force. Those salespeople who *just* reach their targets will receive the sum of $6,350 in incentive payments, in exactly the manner set down in the budget. The selection of caps will be as follows:

Component 1

Quarterly

The cap will be established at 110 per cent. It is desirable that this particular cap should not be too high, as its basic purpose is to try to emphasize total year-end sales. The YTD figure at the end of the planning year is the point at which the most obvious 'potential reward' ought to be located. This is a necessary condition, because if we permit sales to be carried forward towards the total year-end target (as we must), then high performers will not be penalized, but will in fact have the opportunity to earn even greater rewards at the end of the year. This suggests that there is little risk that early caps will prove to be dissatisfiers as they are not really true ceilings. Rather, they are payments that are deferred until the individuals' performance over the year justifies their payment. In this sense, they act to sustain performance levels until the end of the year. If effort drops off, then the salespeople involved lose the benefit of their early work.

Caps used in this way also have other organizational advantages:

1   They help to retain individual members of the sales force over the course of the year. High performers, for example, will certainly want to realize the rewards due to them for their efforts and will remain at least until the YTD incentive is paid.
2   By the third quarter, it will be relatively simple to estimate the level of year-end payouts with a high degree of accuracy – a point that will be appreciated by the accountant.

Some quarterly plans permit a carryover from quarter to quarter. This is certainly an alternative method that could be considered. This approach, however, does not usually have a separate year-end payout, and in this respect it lacks the advantages of the first method.

YTD
This cap will be set at 130 per cent. At this level it is relatively simple to structure payments to ensure that 'all-round' high

performers will have achieved a payout approximating the figure of $16,000. Where certain individuals exceed this level with no apparent market conditions to explain their success, then they should be treated separately. This may involve action other than simply paying an incentive.

Component 2

For the special product campaign, each quarterly effort will be capped at 110 per cent. It will be appreciated that no separate annual payout is necessary here, as these sales add in to Component 1. Two good reasons exist for capping the special product scheme early:

1 It is not desirable to encourage excessive 'loading' in any one quarter against the following quarter. The fact that a different product will be emphasized in the next quarter, with a different incentive structure, is a factor that will have been taken into account when the plan was established.
2 Any higher sales will automatically be allocated to the annual (year-end) incentive.

Component 3

No 'above target' considerations apply in this case.

Lump sums, incentive amounts and 'accelerated' payments

Lump sums

A lump sum awarded when a salesperson achieves the targets set down for them (i.e. 100 per cent) is an excellent means of directing attention to this measurable and desirable objective. The impact of the award is immediate and overt. Individuals receiving the lump sum award gains recognition for their efforts in a very tangible fashion and this can have the effect of motivating their peers to emulate their success. Other members of the sales force who are close to achieving their own targets will be inclined to invest the additional effort necessary to reach the goal, so that in turn they, too, gain recognition for their success.

From an organizational point of view, lump sum payments have profitability implications that should be noted. Those sales people who only achieve 98 per cent of their target, do *not* get 98 per cent of the incentive payments that the 100 per cent performer receives. Their reward in fact will be considerably lower. Once this fact becomes apparent to them, then the 'urge to succeed' is stimulated considerably, since the marginal increase in performance results in a disproportionate gain. It is also possible that towards the end of a planning year, the lump sum payment may have retention value.

Critics of lump sum payments made to salespeople achieving 100 per cent of the targets set down for them, argue that payments of this nature can result in a significantly greater expenses burden between the 99 and 101 per cent levels of sales budget. It is suggested that if enough representatives qualify for the reward by *just* reaching the 100 per cent target level, then the business could be less profitable at 101 per cent of budget, than it would be at 99 per cent.

This argument ignores the fact that the last 1 per cent of sales (in excess of 100 per cent), incurs minimal incremental expenses as all fixed expenses are covered once the targets have been reached. Furthermore, the probability that *every* member of the sales force will *just* reach the 100 per cent level is somewhat remote. What is much more likely to happen in reality is a more or less even distribution of achievement around the 100 per cent level in the form of a normal curve. A distribution of this nature would more likely produce a *saving* for the company, a fact that will be demonstrated as the example proceeds. Note, too, that the term lump sum does not necessarily mean cash.

In both Components 1 and 2 of the plan, lump sum payments will be utilized as follows:

Component 1 (quarterly)

90–99% of target	$40 per %
100% 'hit'	$240 lump sum

Component 1 (year-end)

90–99% of target	$40 per %
100% 'hit'	$240 lump sum

Alternatively, one could grade an achievement level of 90–94 per cent, as being different from 95–99 per cent. One could then accelerate slightly and leave a lump sum of $150 at 100 per cent.

Component 2

80–89% of target	$15 per %
90–99% of target	$25 per %
100% 'hit'	$137.50 lump sum

Incentive amounts and 'accelerated' payouts

The amount of money paid out as incentive, to the point where the salesperson's target is reached, represents a simple mathematical calculation based on the level at which payments begin, how much money is available and how much of this will be set aside for lump sum rewards.

There is considerable agreement among practising managers that the rate at which incentive payments are made should gradually increase as achievement increases, especially if the sales targets are exceeded. Valid reasons exist for this view. First, keep in mind that the incentive that is paid is a reward for achievement. It is paid (and only paid) when a salesperson reaches a particular level of success. This means that each new level of achievement can be symbolized very graphically and given greater emphasis by offering a new and more desirable level of reward. Second, much more freedom of action exists for incentive payments related to above target achievement. The level of incentive offered should be established on the basis of:

(a) What will be considered to be reasonable and attractive to the members of the sales force.
(b) The manager's opinion of the value of sales above budget to the firm.

In the example being developed, accelerated payments will be used as set out below:

Component 1

Quarterly

90–99% of target	$40 per %
100% 'hit'	$240 lump sum
101–110% of target	$70 per %

Year-end

90–99% of target	$40 per %
100% 'hit'	$240 lump sum
101–110% of target	$70 per %
111–120% of target	$120 per %
121–130% of target	$200 per %

Component 2

80–89% of target	$15 per %
90–99% of target	$25 per %
100% 'hit'	$137.50 lump sum
101–110% of target	$50 per %

Table 3 sets out an estimate of payout schedules for four different levels of (consistent) performance.

Notice that in each quarter, there is a marked difference in the level of reward for different levels of performance. Note, too, that the major 'differential' reward is for above target performance and that this is awarded at the year-end payout.

An examination of Table 3 indicates that the significant increment in remuneration that is displayed is directly linked to performance. At 130 per cent of target, a salesperson is actually earning in the order of 110 per cent of his or her base salary; and more than double the incentive awarded to the 100 per cent target performer.

Table 3 *Schedule – payout estimate (all plans)*

	Performance (consistent) level			
	90%	*100%*	*110%*	*130%*
End September (October)	215	1427.5	2627.5	2627.5
End December (January)	215	1427.5	2627.5	2627.5
End March (April)	215	1427.5	2627.5	2627.5
End June (July)	255	2067.5	3967.5	7167.5
Total	900	6350*	11,850	15,050

* Budgeted incentive as part of total compensation.

An alternative approach to over-budget awards

Sketched graphically, an incentive plan for an individual salesperson is set out below (Figure 7).

This figure indicates that incentive payments begin at the 85 per cent level of achievement. The introduction of rewards prior to the 100 per cent target level being achieved is designed to whet the salesperson's appetite by indicating the 'potential' that is available for even better rewards. At the 100 per cent level of achievement, a relatively large lump sum

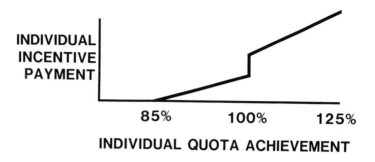

Figure 7

incentive is paid. This is a perfectly logical response to target achievement. Initially, the salesperson's fixation *must* be directed towards the 100 per cent level, because that is the point at which the business achieves all of its objectives. The lump sum award acts to motivate salespeople to exceptional levels of performance and stimulates them to strive for the organization's objectives. The accelerating level of incentive beyond the 100 per cent point results in even greater effort from the sales force, and can be justified because all the fixed costs of the business have now been covered. This being so, then the firm can afford to be generous where extraordinary effort has occurred.

Note that the statements to this point have only been concerned with individual sales achievement and individual sales incentives. Quite clearly, from the organization's viewpoint, a much more relevant concern is for *every* member of the sales force to reach the 100 per cent level of achievement. Total team performance might be improved if the individual payouts were sweetened, conditional upon the sales force *as a whole* achieving, say, 105 or 110 per cent of total target. Figure 8 indicates how this might appear.

For example, at the 105 per cent level of the team's performance, each individual incentive payout (based on 100 per cent performance as set out in the plan) is increased by 25 per cent. If achievement for the whole team reaches 110 per cent (as in Figure 8), then the individual payouts are increased by 50 per cent. The point of this approach is simply that any additional money that is set aside from incremental sales to reward over-budget performance is then distributed among the sales people in proportion to their respective individual performances.

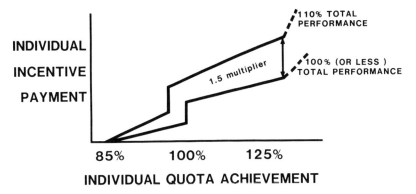

Figure 8

The money could be distributed, of course, on a per capita basis, but this approach would reward those salespeople who underperformed and reached perhaps only 80 per cent of the sales target set down for them. It is possible that some combination of multiplier and per capita distribution might produce better results, giving most to those who achieved most, but at the same time ensuring 100 per cent team interest in over-target performance by giving something to everyone. Travel is a good way of accomplishing this. The team reward is a trip to some exotic centre, but with individuals earning differential cash rewards.

Worksheet 10 will help to resolve the questions raised in this chapter.

Worksheet 10

Plan component	Payment* begins?	Caps?	Carry over?	Accelerated payments?

Consider lump sums.

Note: You might also like to build a payout estimate schedule, similar to that on page 105.

An example of an incentive scheme that failed

A large transport company decided to introduce an incentive scheme to stimulate sales and profits. Their business was focused in three prime areas of activity. 'Express freight', 'large volume general freight' and 'full truckloads on a one-off basis'. Different members of the sales force handled each of these various activities.

The scheme was organized as a contest with salespeople from all areas and all divisions involved. The ground rules were very simple. To become eligible for a prize, a salesperson had to open a minimum of thirty new accounts and generate a minimum of $30,000 *new* revenue over a ten week period. The first prize in each area was $500 in cash plus a new 65 cm colour television set. The second prize was $150, with $100 for the third prize. The prizes went to those salespeople who achieved the highest revenues in each area and who also met the qualifying conditions. To add to the competitiveness of the event, a bar chart displaying each salesperson's results was placed in the foyer of each area office, with the results updated weekly.

The contest was launched at a convention and morale among the sales force was very high. Four weeks later, however, the picture had changed dramatically. It had become fairly obvious that the people selling 'express freight' would easily achieve the thirty new trading accounts to qualify, but not the revenue. Those salespeople charged with selling 'large volume general freight' would achieve the revenue, but not the new accounts. And those people selling 'full truckloads' (one person in each area) to occasional customers (i.e. new accounts), would coast home.

Morale fell away sharply and deep divisions occurred within the sales force. What had previously been a contented and cohesive team was now divided. At the end of the ten week period, only six salespeople out of forty had reached the qualifying level that made it eligible for them to achieve a prize. All of them were 'full truckload' salespeople.

The original purpose of the scheme was to motivate the sales force to generate increased sales and profits. Not only did total sales fall during the period of the contest, but they remained lower than normal for a further seven months, during a particularly buoyant economic period.

SEVEN

Special concerns

The nature of rewards

Before beginning this chapter, the reader should note that Step 9 is still being considered. Reference back to the figure on page 96 will confirm this.

The major categories of reward that are offered in sales incentive programs are cash, travel, goods and entertainment. The last category has its uses, but tends to lack the power of the other three. For this reason, discussion and selection will be focused on the first three categories only.

Cash incentives can certainly be made very 'attractive' to salespeople and properly structured, will be perceived as being 'reasonable'. But the adverse impact of taxation on each person's total compensation (real or perceived) can dampen the attractiveness of the incentive in a great many cases, especially if the rewards that are earned take an individual into a much higher tax bracket. This problem is very real and can radically influence a person's response to the question of how much effort should be invested in relation to the potential rewards that may be earned. In this context, it is interesting to note that in the current industrial climate, trade union officials preparing logs of claims for their members, are increasingly basing their demands on the after tax earnings that their members receive, rather than the gross dollar amounts that are earned.

It should not be forgotten that money is a common symbolic reward that means many things to many people, even though it has become increasingly common over the last decade or so to offer incentives in the form of non-cash awards. Such awards may take the form of shopping vouchers, travel, gifts, or, perhaps, even charge accounts at major stores. It would appear that in many firms, non-cash payments are seen to be a means of easing 'the tax burden' on high earning salespeople, although one wonders why, bearing in mind that most 'benefits in kind' are now fully taxable. It would be just as easy and much more effective to offset tax bracket jumps by using such devices as accelerated payment schedules, or similar financial measures. Governments around the world are becoming increasingly aware of the existence of non-cash awards and the tax implications inherent in them. It is unlikely that they will escape their attention much longer.

From the company's perspective, the major problem with cash incentives is that they all too easily become an expectation on the part of the people receiving them, so that within a short period of time they are perceived to be a 'normal' part of salary expectation. This is especially the case if the awards are paid in a routine fashion, or where the payout periods are really too frequent (e.g. monthly).

Goods can be used to overcome some of the problems that are associated with cash as long as the concepts of attractiveness and reasonableness are kept in mind. If a salesperson's salary is in the vicinity of $20,000 a year, then it is unlikely that he or she will find a $50 appliance devastatingly attractive. By the same token, if a company representative has earned incentives to the value of, say, $15,000, it is unlikely that the gift of a new car will be seen to be reasonable.

A good reason for considering non-cash rewards, however, is in relation to the problem of sustaining high-levels of motivation over time. Attention was drawn earlier to the tendency for cash incentives to become regarded as an integral part of normal salary whenever they are paid on a routine basis. Once this happens, of course, then the incentive does little to stimulate greater effort. And, in fact, the longer the incentive remains in force, the more difficult it will be to withdraw it later. The great advantage of non-cash rewards is that they have considerable flexibility.

Travel tends to have fewer problems associated with it, particularly if it is tied to other corporate objectives. This can be done in a number of ways. The representative, for example, might be required to undertake a survey of new product opportunities at an overseas trade fair, or attend a seminar designed to develop new skills, or perhaps even to examine export opportunities in a new market.

Associated tasks of this nature add to the prestige of the trip and provide additional recognition of the individual's worth to the company. Nevertheless, choice remains important and journeys imposed on the person may not be seen to be attractive or reasonable.

Perhaps the best incentive plans provide a mix of all three. With the need for administrative simplicity kept in mind, in the example being developed, two components only will be used. Cash will be one, because of the breadth of symbolism that is associated with it. And travel will be the other, because of its attractiveness. Tables 4 and 5 indicate how these two categories will be used in Component 1.

Component 1

Table 4   *Quarterly*

Achievement	Rate	Cash	Travel
90–99%	40 per %	Total	—
100% 'hit'	240 (lump sum)	Total	—
101–110%	70 per %	Total	—

Because travel is perceived to be a *highly attractive reward*, it will be saved until the end of the year.

Table 5   *Year-end (total sales)*

Achievement	Rate	Cash	Travel
90–99%	40 per %	Total	—
100% 'hit'	240 (lump sum)	Total	—
101–110%	70 per %	10 per %	60 per %
110–120%	120 per %	40 per %	80 per %
121–130%	200 per %	80 per %	120 per %

Component 2

Cash only will be used for this component.

Worksheet 11 is designed to assist you to allocate different rewards to different components of your incentive plan. Approach the matter critically and keep the motives of the salespeople uppermost in your mind.

Worksheet 11

Cash? Which components? ....

....

....

Goods? Which components? ....

....

....

Travel? Which components? Can something be added

(e.g. educational value)? ....

....

....

Build your own table (e.g. as on page 113). Make sure the rules of *reasonableness* and *attractiveness* are kept in mind as and if you split rewards.

Special concerns for special situations

Sales incentive plans are often compromised because of the presence of unusual issues. Four such issues are discussed here.

New products

New product development and introduction are normal company activities designed to create a competitive advantage. It is obvious, however, that new products will emerge, and will be launched at times that favour *their* success, rather than at times that are convenient for the incentive planner.

One way to handle new products is simply to make note of them as they are wending their way through the new product development process, and integrate them into the design of the incentive plan under development. But, new products invariably have a degree of uncertainty associated with them, and seldom perform as expected. Launch dates are not always met, costs may be higher than anticipated (which may affect the price), and the success of a new product can never be guaranteed. The impact of even one of these problems can act to disturb the even progression of a scheme and in turn, may demotivate the salespeople, who suddenly see their own personal efforts being disrupted by factors outside their control.

For this reason, it is best to exclude new products from a total sales quota incentive plan and to make use of a special product plan that is specifically designed for the new product. This action has the effect of distancing the new product from the 'cash cows' that produce the bulk of current revenue, and establishes it as a separate but specific objective for achievement. As such, it will have its own specific rewards.

Price increases

Some of the problems of setting targets on a dollar basis were discussed in Chapter 3. Incentive plans are designed to sell product units. But if the projected sales of these products are established in dollar figures, then problems will arise not only when trying to compare one year's sales with another as inflation takes its toll, but also whenever price increases occur. The obvious impact that price increases have on incentive plans (unless corrected) is that they produce payouts for the sales force that do *not* reflect the true performance of the salespeople involved.

A firm's budgets and targets are set on the basis of certain assumptions, one of which is price. If significant changes occur to any one of these assumptions, then it will probably be necessary to restate the targets (up or down) that the sales-people are working towards. Incentive schemes must be fairly structured. If the sales force are working towards targets that are set too low, or impossible to achieve, then motivation will suffer. The first does an injustice to the firm, the second leads to dissatisfaction among the salespeople.

If changes have to be made to the targets that have been agreed, then there is a very real need for them to be well-communicated. Of course, a prerequisite for successful communication is that the basis of the incentive scheme should be thoroughly understood by the salesforce beforehand. It has to be stressed that great care is needed whenever targets are manipulated up or down. If an individual has worked hard and the target is suddenly lowered, then that person's sense of achievement is taken away from him or her. The same is true of targets that are too high. Even a donkey will refuse to follow a carrot that constantly moves away.

Also, there appears to be a mistaken belief among some managers that manipulating the targets up and down somehow represents 'good psychology' and keeps the sales force on their toes. One could well ask: 'Good psychology for whom?' In fact, a very good decision rule to work with is to set the targets on the basis of a sober appraisal of totally realistic possibilities, *the sum of which is equal to budgeted sales.* The practice of overstating targets for each of the salespeople by some percentage to 'guarantee' that the total sales target is met, is somewhat childish. If objectives have been properly set and sound plans have been developed to achieve them, then it is silly to confuse matters with exaggerations.

Managing 'high achievers'

Concern is often expressed at senior management level when large incentive payouts are made to high achievers. It may become a particularly sensitive issue when the total remuneration of high achievers exceeds that of certain senior staff. In essence, however, the concern is perceived to be related to profit considerations, and to the possible affect on morale if overall the sales team fail to achieve their objectives, but one or two of them far exceed their individual targets. One can explore the impact of such an event by exploring it in the example that is currently being developed.

Let us suppose, then, that the total sales objective has been clearly missed, say, by a factor of 20 per cent (i.e. 80 per cent of target). Let us also suppose that two members of the sales team both achieved 130 per cent of target. Given this situation, one would suppose that even the most cynical of managers would regard it as inappropriate *not* to reward these high achievers for their efforts. After all, if these people had not performed as well as they did, then the business would be in an even worse shape than it is.

Note that the cost of rewarding the high achievers is

$30,100. The amount that the firm budgeted for 100 per cent achievement was $63,500. The question that now has to be resolved is very straightforward. Is the payment of 47 per cent of the amount set down for incentive payments too high for an achievement level of 80 per cent (see Table 6)? Note, too, that if the other eight salespeople (who fell short of their targets) had received their collection incentives, the payout would still only be 60 per cent of the incentive money set down for this purpose, or 88 per cent of budgeted total compensation.

Developing the logic of this exercise a little further, one is obliged to ask what the impact on profitability would be, if, say, five of the representatives achieved 130 per cent of target, but the total sales force achievement was only 90 per cent? Well, it has to be recognized that the probability of this happening is very low and to gain the high levels of motivation that results from a good incentive plan, some element of risk has to be accepted. In a real situation, what is most likely to happen is not a bunching of identical outcomes, but rather spread of results. This is illustrated in Table 6, using Components 1 and 2 as examples.

Table 6

Representative	Quota achievement (assumed consistent)	Incentive payment
1	78%	0
2	95%	2100
3	100%	5300
4	110%	10,850
5	130%	14,050
6	105%	8100
7	98%	3300
8	95%	2100
9	90%	900
10	83%	180
Average	100%	Total 46,930

If we make the assumption that the sales territories are of equal size, then the achievement of 100 per cent of budgeted sales will result in an incentive payout of $46,930, against a planned budget of $53,500 for Components 1 and 2. This is a very realistic situation. Note, too, that if lump sum payments had not been utilized, then representatives 2, 7, 8 and 9 (at least), would have received *additional* payouts! There is certainly a risk that profits at 101 per cent of budgeted sales might be less than at 99 per cent, but this is a risk that should be accepted as the cost of stimulating sales beyond the 101 per cent point.

Retail selling

Managers in retail situations often claim that incentive plans are not suitable for salespeople working in a retail environment. Typically it is argued that:

(a) Retail salespeople do not control their leads. They simply wait for people to walk into the store.
(b) It is not possible to set clear targets in a store setting. They are affected too much by the actions of the buyers and the prices that competitors are offering.
(c) Information on individual sales is not available.

Responses to these claims are fairly clear-cut.

Point (a) is simply an excuse. There is little difference between the retail store and the external environment. All salespeople have the opportunity to influence their own results by making good use of the promotional backing that is provided for them and retail salespeople have precisely the same opportunities. They can influence not only who comes into the store, but more importantly, who comes back. In addition, they can influence the stores merchandising policy and also the size of the orders that are placed. Since people entering the store do so in a buying frame of mind (or they wouldn't be there), then the salesperson has the opportunity to indulge in some creative personal selling. They can persuade people to come again, and perhaps even to bring their friends.

Point (b) also lacks validity. Targets can be set in many different ways. They can be set daily, weekly, monthly, quarterly or annually. The tendency, however, is for incentive periods to be fairly short in the retail context. Even so, it is not that difficult to specify that certain quantities of stock will be moved over certain periods of time. And points targets can be used to weight specific merchandise, as a means of emphasizing the direction of selling effort.

Point (c) is easily solved. The store simply needs to instal a modern POS cash register system.

EIGHT

Communicating the incentive plan

Developing an incentive plan is a time-consuming activity that involves many days of work to produce a worthwhile result. A really good plan that is responsive to the firm's objectives is a major task that will involve a number of people for long periods of time. Some sales managers *are* aware of the time investment necessary to write a good incentive plan. Even so, they may fail to recognize the need to devote a comparative amount of time to the task of communicating the outcome of their planning to the people who will be most affected by it.

It is a simple fact of business that it doesn't matter how good the final plan appears to be if the incentives are not visible and well understood by the salespeople, or if they do not understand or accept the targets that have been set down for them, or if the rewards are not well communicated to them – then the scheme is doomed to failure.

An incentive scheme *has* to be well communicated to the sales force if it is to work and the positive aspects of the scheme must be understood and accepted *if* the scheme is to be successful. Some points that will help to introduce a scheme to the salespeople are set out below:

- A good plan is a simple plan, that has no unnecessary complications built into it. Since it is not possible to achieve every desirable business objective in the course of a single planning year, it is necessary to isolate the *priority* business objectives that *must* be achieved. This activity will serve to reduce the number of separate objectives that have to be addressed, which in turn, will minimize the number of rewards that need to be established. Complicated schemes inevitably lead to problems and demotivation. If complicated formulas begin to emerge, then there is a need to pause, and question whether a simpler approach might not be better.

- Explain the plan verbally to the salespeople and reinforce it at regular intervals throughout the year. The annual sales meeting is the proper place to unveil the scheme and reinforcement can be undertaken at the regular sales meetings (monthly?) as the year goes by. When a new incentive scheme is being explained, always allow sufficient time for the salespeople to ask questions, so that they can satisfy themselves about the details of the scheme. Test for *acceptance, understanding* and *commitment*, noting that the three are different. Testing for understanding, for example, means putting relevant questions to the salespeople, to test their perception of the scheme itself. Testing for commitment means measuring the degree of dissatisfaction that is present.

- Provide a written description of the plan, or perhaps even invest in an attractive brochure that details the objectives and the rewards. Encourage the salespeople to retain the details for future reference. Include charts or worksheets in the written description, on which individuals can log their targets and keep an on-going record of their performance.

If the rewards that have been built into the incentive plan are to have a positive impact on each person's performance, then frequent feedback and reinforcement are necessary. Feedback should be provided on at least a monthly basis, so that each salesperson knows how well he or she is performing against the targets that he or she has to achieve. This is equally important where team targets have been set and a group of salespeople are striving to reach a team or district incentive.

Feedback should be related to the targets that have to be achieved. For example, if the plan offers rewards in respect of:

1 Total sales (quarterly).
2 Total sales (year-end).
3 Quarterly sales of Product X.
4 The reduction of accounts receivable.

Then each salesperson should receive at least four items of information. Once they have this basic data, then it becomes possible for each of them to chart their progress, thus bringing the achievement motive into play. An additional piece of information that would certainly assist the salespeople would be the total results for the whole team. With this information, they could not only compare their own results with their own targets, but could also identify their own contribution to the firm's objectives. Readers will remember from Chapter 2 that the opportunity to make a contribution can be a motivational factor for many individuals. Others, of course, may see their own personal achievement versus others, as a means of satisfying their competitive drive. But care is needed not to overload the feedback channel with large quantities of quantitative data, computer printouts and other unnecessary material. The salespeople should be provided with sufficient data for them to track their own performance, but not enough to bore them.

Use Worksheet 12 to help plan how your plan will be communicated to the sales force.

Worksheet 12

Review your plan. Is it *simple*? Are the rewards directly traceable to the key objectives?

....

....

Plan to communicate:

When: ....

....

How: ....

....

What visual support: ....

....

What handout support? ....

....

Feedback plan:

Frequency: ....

....

Required detail: ....

....

Can salespeople keep ongoing record? How? What will each need?

....

....

An example of a well communicated plan

An excellent example of a well explained plan took the form of a cheque book with a typical bank cover. It contained a written explanation, together with a recording capability (which is, of course, how a cheque book works). Each page of the 'cheque book' represented a potential incentive payout with the corresponding record form, permitted targets and achievements to be documented. This particular format had very good novelty value and made the rewards that could be earned very obvious. It also permitted the representatives to keep a record of their progressive achievement and helped to keep the scheme alive throughout the year.

PART 3

Miscellaneous worksheets

Two miscellaneous worksheets are included in this Part. You are invited to review their usefulness to your own situation. They have proved useful in helping managers confront quarterly break-out of targets and the mix-and-match of individual representative's probable achievement to the total company target.

Miscellaneous Worksheet A

Objective	1st quarter	2nd quarter	3rd quarter	4th quarter	Year

Miscellaneous Worksheet B

% of target

Representative or area	25	50	75	100	125	150
Total company target						

Index